Proceeding On

Tim Walter

Learn more about this book and its
author by visiting our web site:

www.overboardministries.com

ISBN: 0983456887
ISBN-13: 978-0-9834568-8-9

Cover design by Innovative Graphics
www.igprodesign.com

This title is available for your favorite eReader. Visit
our web site to choose the format
that's right for you.

All comments or requests for
information should be sent to:
overboard@overboardministries.com

DEDICATION

This book is dedicated to the seven most important people in my life: my wife Sarah and our six children, Anders, Aidan, Abigail, Autumn, Annie and Alistair. I could have no greater accomplishment in life than the knowledge that I am loved so gracefully and deeply by you all. May the many future adventures in life lead us into a closer walk with Jesus, as we "proceed on" through the journey of life. To my wife Sarah, there are not enough words to express how wonderful you are. Thank you for your unconditional love for me and for your amazing and awe-inspiring commitment to our children's rearing. To my children, you all are examples to me in many ways, and your dad learns a lot from you all...

Anders...your creativity and determination
Aidan...your humor and joyfulness
Abigail...your simplicity and kindness
Autumn...your independence and grit
Annie...your playfulness and spunk
Alistair...your peacefulness and tranquility

EXPLANATION

The text for the journal entries is taken from Bernard DeVoto's condensed version of the original journals. As the reader will notice, the spelling and grammar would not be acceptable in today's world. I did not revise them because the actual writings added an authenticity to the entries. I say we cut Lewis and Clark a break with their spelling and grammar; after all, we are talking about two men with some gunpowder and ink that changed the history of the nation forever.

FOREWORD BY THE AUTHOR

I remember, as a kid growing up in South Dakota, seeing an old bumper sticker from the Little Bighorn National Battlefield on one of the rusty cabinets in our garage. Every time I would walk past it, I would see the pictures of Custer and Sitting Bull, and my imagination would take over.

Before long, I was running around playing cowboys and Indians. Then, when we moved to the Northeast, my father took us to historical places: Gettysburg, Independence Hall, Jamestown, Williamsburg, Ellis Island; the list goes on. History has always been an interest of mine.

But it is a love of the history of the American West that has captivated me above all else. I have never given up that boyhood dream of riding a horse through the wilds of the west. I realize now that God was speaking to me through that bumper sticker, and that interest led to what you are about to read.

About four years ago, after returning from eight years serving the Lord in Russia, that old flame was rekindled. I picked up Stephen Ambrose's book "Undaunted Courage" about the Lewis and Clark expedition. I was enthralled. I read it twice in a few months. From there, I read a condensed version of the journals of Lewis and Clark. Again, I was captivated, but this time it was for a different, and much more important, reason. I found myself reading through the journals, stopping often to think about how my walk with Jesus was similar to the adventures those men were having. I started reading my Bible along with the journals, highlighting similarities.

Jesus was revealing Himself more and more to me, as I read His word along with the journals. After some time, I began to record what Jesus was teaching me through His word and paralleling that with examples from Lewis and Clark's journals. Thus birthed the idea of what you are about to read.

Two things are worthy to mention. I am not a historian by any means. If for any reason I have misrepresented anything from a historical aspect of the Corps of Discovery, it is my fault alone. Often my thoughts are simply speculations of how Lewis and Clark must have been feeling. Also, when dealing with metaphors, I have tried very carefully not to take any Scripture out of context. If for any reason I have, once again it is my fault alone, and I rely on the Holy Spirit to show the readers any faults therein.

As amazing as Lewis and Clark's expedition was, it cannot compete with the adventure offered by a relationship with Jesus Christ. The greatest day in my life was when I declared Him my Savior, and I am so humbled that He could take my interest, a love for history, and allow me to use it for His glory.

My hope for this devotional is that He would be glorified and that you, the readers, will be inspired as you travel with Lewis and Clark. I hope you are spurred to chase the dreams God has placed on your hearts -- even if they come in the form of a bumper sticker in a garage!

Most of all, I hope that, above all, this devotional may draw you closer to Jesus, help you grasp the amazing love He has for you and encourage you to share the Gospel with others.

AMAZINGLY UNQUALIFIED

"Of courage undaunted, possessing a firmness and perseverance of purpose which nothing but impossibilities could diver from it's direction, careful as a father of those committed to his charge,yet steady in the maintenance of order and discipline, intimate with the Indian character, customs, and principles, habituated to the hunting life, guarded by exact observation of the vegetables and animals of his own country, against losing time in the description of objects already possessed, honest, disinterested, liberal, of sound understanding and fidelity to truth so scrupulous that whatever he should report would be as certain as if seen by ourselves, with all these qualifications as if selected and implanted by nature in one body, for this purpose, I could have no hesitation in confiding the enterprise to him." *Thomas Jefferson, 1813*

When it came to being qualified for the job of leading the Corps of Discovery, the words of Thomas Jefferson tell whether Meriwether Lewis "had what it would take" to lead the monumental expedition. We cannot read this commendation of the man Lewis without realizing with certainty that President Jefferson deemed him most qualified. What a list of qualifications he had! Jefferson had a lot riding on this expedition, and he took careful concern to select the man who would lead it. He needed the best of the best to pull it off.

"God has chosen the foolish things of the world to shame the wise, and God has chosen the weak things of the world to shame the things which are strong." 1 Corinthians 1:27

1

When we think of this concept of "being qualified for the task" as it relates to us and the task Jesus gives us, we are forced to realize a hard truth: we are not qualified. We fail; our track record is miserable in many areas, but, despite this, Jesus desires to entrust us with the ministry He has given us. Paul tells us that in the verse above.

Oh, how amazing a God we serve! He actually looks for the "rough cuts" in the lot! He looks at our weaknesses as opportunities for Him to shine in us! Is it not amazing that God in His infinite knowledge knows how unqualified we are for what He asks us to do...and then He willingly desires to entrust us anyway? It is His work on the cross at Calvary that does the qualifying for us!

President Jefferson would not dare pick a rough cut to lead the Corps of Discovery, while we have a God who intentionally *chooses* the rough cuts to present Him to a hurting world. Amazing! What a privilege to be unqualified for the task at hand! For, in our lack of qualification, He shines forth.

Questions for Reflection:

1. How should your "unqualification" empower you to live for Christ more passionately?

2. What does this show you about God's character?

3. How can the truths found in this devotional be lived out in your life today?

FIRST IMPRESSIONS

"In all your intercourse with the natives treat them in the most friendly & conciliatory manner which their own conduct will admit." Thomas Jefferson in his instructional letter to Lewis

First impressions were a big thing for the expedition. Jefferson realized that the Missouri River was a key trade route for the future, and he also knew that a bunch of native tribes called the banks of the river their home. Therefore, it was key that Lewis and Clark set a good relational foundation for future traders, expeditions, etc. All rested on those often tense first impressions.

"Conduct yourselves with wisdom toward outsiders, making the most of the opportunity." Colossians 4:5

Often life is about first impressions. This is magnified when it comes to the witness we are to the world as followers of Jesus. Too many people have turned from God simply because of impressions they have had from the often ungodly behaviors and attitudes of those who bear the name of Christ.

If we could understand that every encounter we have with every person could be viewed as an eternal encounter for that person, how much would our behavior change? Through our actions, speech, and motives, we have the ability to draw people close to Jesus or push them farther away. What a wonderful opportunity! What a dreadful warning!

May people be drawn to Jesus through the lives they see us live. May our actions towards outsiders compel them to know the God we speak about! May we shudder in fear at the thought of our actions being a deterrent in drawing a person to the grace of God!

Questions for Reflection:

1. How should the first impressions you make as a follower of Jesus differ from the world's impressions?

2. When it comes to the first impressions you give to others, how would you say you come across?

3. How can the truths found in this devotional be lived out in your life today?

INFORMATION LOST

"In the loss of yourselves, we should lose also the information you will have acquired." Thomas Jefferson in his instructional letter to Lewis

The journals of Lewis and Clark had to be preserved, for within them was held a whole new undiscovered frontier. Jefferson asked them to send back journals at different times in their journey to ensure they would not be lost. Jefferson feared that all the information would be lost if the men perished; the journey was so valuable that he commanded them to return if their lives were in jeopardy and no other option seemed available, so the journals would not be lost. The journals would become a legacy of the American frontier.

> *"According to my earnest expectation and hope,*
> *that I shall not be put to shame in anything, but*
> *that with all boldness, Christ shall even now, as*
> *always, be exalted in my body, whether by life or*
> *by death." Philippians 1:20*

One day, we will die. It is a fact we share with every person on earth. The question we must ask ourselves is what has our life done on this earth for the further glorification of Jesus Christ? It should sadden us that many Christians die without ever leaving a Christ-glorifying legacy on earth.

We go through the motions, but never view our lives through the perspective of eternal glory. We were put on this earth to glorify Christ, as Paul stated, "whether by life or death." This is why, when the Lord calls us home at His appointed time for us, we must be ready to exit this earth with a certainty that the way we have lived will leave a Christ-exalting legacy, a life that people can look to and see the goodness of the Savior.

5

Our lives are "letters from Christ" (2 Corinthians 3:2-3), and we do not have to worry as Jefferson did that all the things we have done for Christ will be lost when we die. No information will be lost, for our life's legacy should be one thing at the end: the glorification of Jesus Christ.

Questions for Reflection:

1. How Christ-exalting is the legacy you are presently preparing to leave behind on this earth?

2. Is Christ being exalted in your life as He should be? If not, what areas can you work on?

3. How can the truths found in this devotional be lived out in your life today?

CONNECTING

"The object of your mission is to explore the Missouri river, and such principal stream of it, as, it's course and commmunication with the waters of the Pacific Ocean, may offer the most direct and practicable water communication across this continent, for the purpose of commerce." Thomas Jefferson, June 20, 1803

This was the charge President Jefferson gave to Meriwhether Lewis: try and find the way to connect the Missouri River and the Pacific Ocean; find the infamous Northwest Passage. Connect the two, and then commerce will flourish. Sadly, as history shows, the dream of finding an all-water route from the Missouri to the Pacific died when they found the source of the Missouri in Montana. The Missouri and the Pacific would *never* be connected.

> *"But God, being rich in mercy, because of His great love with which He loved us, even when we were dead in our transgressions, made us alive together with Christ (by grace you have been saved)." Ephesians 2:4*

In the end, life is about connecting two things: a perfect, holy, loving God and an imperfect, unholy, selfish, lost man. After that fateful day when sin came into the garden, life took a drastic turn for man. He had fallen from the very thing he was supposed to be connected with: his soul. It became disconnected from God.

This is the real problem and issue all men face today, one they have faced since that day in the garden. The soul of man cries out from deep within, "Oh, how I long to be connected to God!" The question asked is, "Oh, how can I return to the source of life?" And it is in the sinful state of man that the question is answered by selfish ambition. The soul says, "I can attain this! I can through my own efforts and strivings reconnect with God."

And like all efforts of an imperfect being trying to earn the love and merit of God, we fail. Every time. The connection must come from God first, and it has come, in the life, death, and resurrection of Jesus Christ. The problem of the disconnect has been solved! It is the gift of God to man. On the cross the holy Savior cries out, "I have done this for you. I have reconnected with you, not you with me." Me with you, not you with me. There is power in that statement. God did it all in Christ Jesus' death. The connection has been made.

Questions for Reflection:

1. What does the truth that Jesus connected us to God mean to you?

2. Have you ever tried the world's ways to connect to God?

3. How can the truths found in this devotional be lived out in your life today?

SERVANT

"Here my Servent York Swam to the Sand bar to geather Greens for our dinner, and retunred with a sufficent quantity wild Creases or Tung grass." William Clark, June 5, 1804

One of the unsung heroes of the expedition was Clark's personal slave, a man named York. He proved just as capable, if not more capable, than all the men of the expedition, and yet, sadly, he received no compensation for his efforts, as did the other men. It was a sad stain on the times back then, that a man could own another. Although he was a slave, York was also a true servant, who gave up much to serve Clark.

"Peter said to Him, 'Never shall You wash my feet!' Jesus answered him, 'If I do not wash you, you have no part with Me.'" John 13:8

The reason we can confidently put others before us and serve them is because that is what Jesus did for us. As a leader, He led by serving. By doing this, He gave us the truth that He was about His Father's business, and He desired to do what the Father desired. It was not fair that He came to serve. If anything, He had every right to punish, but that is not what He did. Rather than come to punish, He came to serve. It was the power of His serving that humbled man.

This is what Peter could not comprehend when Jesus desired to wash his feet. Jesus was showing a pivotal truth in the life of the Christian: if you desire to walk closely and identify with Jesus, you must serve others. You must lay down your desires for those of others.

Unlike Clark's servant York, who had no choice in being a servant because of the terrible and accepted institution of slavery that existed, Jesus chose to put Himself in that place; He became a servant to those who would later abandon Him and rebel against Him. Oh, the amazing servant love of God!

Questions for Reflection:

1. In what areas of your life can you become a better servant?

2. How can the truth that Jesus came as a servant be an example in your daily life?

3. How can the truths found in this devotional be lived out in your life today?

DEN OF RATTLESNAKES

"We landed at this Inscription and found it a Den of RattleSnakes, we had not landed 3 Minities before three verry large Snakes was observed in the Crevises of the rocks & killed." William Clark, June 7, 1804

The expedition was filled with dangers. Although only one person on the expedition lost his life, the Corps of Discovery found themselves in many situations that could have proven fatal. The above entry was written at the very beginning of the expedition. Just like that, one wrong move around a bunch of rattlesnakes could have taken someone's life. With the constant dangers from weather, animals, Indians, and accidents, the understanding of how fragile life was must have been understood by all.

"So teach us to number our days, That we may present to You a heart of wisdom." Psalm 90:12

We never know when death will come. David teaches us an important truth. Our days are numbered, and every day is a gift of grace from God, to be spent in ways that glorify Him.

What if every morning when we arise, our first thought would be that the day we have is a gift of grace? What if we were aware that it might be the last one we have on earth? How would we live differently? What motives would drive our decisions and actions?

Many "rattlesnakes" in the world try to take our lives: selfishness, greed, lust, wrong motives, grudges. These are all life-threatening to our spirits. Death does not just mean we stop breathing; it means we slowly begin to suffocate our spirits with the things of the world rather than nourish them with the things of God.

To number our days means to live at such a godly standard that not a breath is wasted in pushing toward the glorification of Jesus Christ in our lives.

Questions for Reflection:

1. If today were your last on earth, could you say you finished well?

2. How should David's words spur you on to live a more Christ-exalting life?

3. How can the truths found in this devotional be lived out in your life today?

SNAGS

"We got fast on a Snag Soon after we Set out which detained us a Short time." William Clark, June 9, 1804

As the expedition struggled upstream, the men were constantly plagued by their canoes hanging up on snags of submerged trees and logs in the Missouri River. The frustration these must have caused is hard to imagine. The snags damaged the boats, which needed repairs, which caused time to be lost in the progression of the expedition. Snags, although annoying and troublesome, were unfortunately part of the journey.

"But I say, walk by the Spirit, and you will not carry out the desire of the flesh." Galatians 5:16

As we mature in Christ, snags will always deter us. Whether it be the daily challenges that life brings from a tight financial time or an unexpected sickness, we cannot eliminated these snags; they come with life. We must allow God to guide us through them and trust Him because He has allowed these snags to affect our lives.

The more dangerous snags are those we bring on ourselves, those snags that were never intended to hinder our walk with Jesus, but, because of our selfish ways or bad decisions, they come nonetheless. These snags are dangerous. They come in the form of things like a bitter heart, unforgiveness or a critical spirit. These will always hinder our growth in Christ, and we must make a conscious decision to recognize them on the horizon and steer clear.

We need to embrace the snags of life that come, but we must not create them. The answer to not creating them is to walk in the Spirit, which has been abundantly given to us.

13

Questions for Reflection:

1. Why would God put "snags" in your life?

2. What "snags" do you often see on the horizon that you need to choose to steer clear of in your daily life?

3. How can the truths found in this devotional be lived out in your life today?

SEASONS

"At this season the Indians on this river are in the Praries hunting the Buffalow." William Clark, July 23, 1804

The tribes of the Great Plains were dependent upon the different seasons to survive. Their daily lives were structured based on the season they were in. Lewis and Clark would often arrive at a village to find most of the men gone on hunting expeditions. Whether it was hunting when the herds were moving or making clothing and resting in the winter, the seasons were times of learning and preparing.

> *"There is an appointed time for everything, And there is a time for every event under heaven."*
> *Ecclesiastes 3:1*

There are hard seasons in a Christian's walk, but there are never bad seasons when we look at them through the eyes of sanctification. When we look at the seasons of life as seasons that are meant to refine us to become more like Jesus, then all of them are good, even though they may come with terrible cost and pain.

Seasons are not quick things; they are lengthy, and they are key to the sustaining of life. Spring's rain allows summer's crops to bear fruit, which allows fall's soils to become fertile for the next year, while winter replenishes the soil with needed rest.

The seasons are vital for the growth of the crop. That's what God does with us when He gives us good seasons, hard seasons, confusing seasons, and seasons filled with happiness or sadness. They are meant for His greater purposes and for us to continue the adventure of becoming more like Christ. We need to embrace the season we find ourselves in with the eyes of sanctification. We will find that the only way to enter that season we desire is to yield to the lessons He is trying to teach us in the season we are presently in.

Questions for Reflection:

1. Think of the many seasons of life the Lord has brought you through. What are some of the reasons He brought you through them?

2. Why is it healthy for you to have many seasons in life?

3. How can the truths found in this devotional be lived out in your life today?

LIFE OF OBSCURITY

"Serjeant Floyd is taken verry bad all at once with a Biliose Chorlick. We attempt to relive him without success as yet, he gets worst and we are much allarmed at his Situation, all attention to him." William Clark, August 19, 1804

Charles Floyd died a day after this entry; he would be the only member of the expedition to perish. He died from what is believed to be appendicitis. His death came early and hit the men hard. Although given full military honors, Floyd's name is often simply remembered as "the one who died." Because he died so early in the expedition, it is easy to pass over his life and see it lost in the pages of history. He was not able to make a name on the expedition, as his journey was cut short. When the men reached the Pacific, they all left their names in the pages of history, but Floyd was a name lost in obscurity.

> *"And they said, 'Come, let us build for ourselves a city and tower whose top will reach into heaven, and let us make a name for ourselves...'" Genesis 11:4*

Deep within the heart of man is the dark desire to be recognized and to draw attention to the accomplishments of self. Like a cancer that never goes away, so is the desire to be recognized. This desire can be as loud as a thunderstorm, demanding everyone around to take notice. It also can be as quiet as a still breeze, for no one to recognize but ourselves, which is equally as dangerous, as this also has the stench of pride and accomplishment of self.

What if we were to live our lives with the understanding that we would never be recognized for anything at all? No accomplishments; no grand goals achieved; no names to be spoken of for years to come. What if we were content to live in obscurity and simply rejoice in the understanding that we are loved by God and that He, and He alone, notices our deeds? That should be enough.

Will we rejoice in a life of Christ-exalting obscurity? Will we find contentment without man's recognition, but with full recognition of the Father?

Questions for Reflection:

1. How much do you desire to get recognition for the things you do?

2. How should your desire to be recognized by Christ alone affect your daily life?

3. How can the truths found in this devotional be lived out in your life today?

DOING WHAT WE LIKE

"Having for many days past confined myself to the boat, I determined to devote this day to amuse myself on shore with my gun and view the interior of the country..." Meriwhether Lewis, September 17, 1804

Lewis decided it was time for some R and R. He jumped off the boat with his gun, dog and ambition to simply have fun and spend the day doing what he wanted to. Maybe he decided to take a breather from being in charge and do something he always loved to do for leisure. Those times probably were a life-line for him, considering the great stress he was under during the entire expedition.

> *"Delight yourself in the Lord; and He will give you the desires of your heart." Psalm 37:4*

The last thing the church needs is more "religious" people, doing "religious" things to look spiritual, while at the same time they are plagued inside by the monotony of their shallow, stale lifestyles.

When was the last time you pondered the idea that it glorifies God when we do things we enjoy? Too many times, we wrap ourselves up in superficial Christian service, trying to give the impression that it is those things that give us the most fulfillment and draw us nearer to God, when, in truth, they are usually the things that drain us and keep us from God!

Do we not realize the desires of our heart were put there by a God whose heart is made glad when He sees His children doing the things they enjoy? This is where we cross over from worship being a thing we do every now and then to a lifestyle we live, because we worship Him in everything. What a privilege to be able to go on a hike, take a jog, paint a picture or simply watch the stars at night and have those things that we enjoy usher us into His powerful presence! Do the things you enjoy; they were put there by God. When you do them, understand that He is glorified by our enjoyment of the pleasures He has blessed us with.

Questions for Reflection:

1. Take time to think of the things you love to do. Have you been able to view them as a way to worship God?

2. In what ways can the wrong motives for Christian service affect you?

3. How can the truths found in this devotional be lived out in your life today?

IMPRESSING OTHERS

"Capt Lewis Shewed them the air Gun. Shot it several times." Sgt. John Orway, September 25, 1804

The Teton Sioux were a feared tribe along the Missouri River. If at any point in the expedition the men expected trouble, it was with them. One of the ways that Lewis and Clark tried to deter the Sioux from attacking them was simply by impressing them with their firepower, by firing their guns. This impressive display was meant not only to impress the Sioux, but also to subtly warn them of their power should the Sioux decide to attack.

> *"For they loved the approval of men rather than the approval of God." John 12:43*

Man is impressed by all things that glorify himself: his achievements, his doings, his ideas. It is not hard to impress man, because we are so futile and selfish, but these do not impress God. God cannot work with a man who desires to please men more than to please Him.

This is where Saul went wrong: he desired the praise of man above all else. This is where Joseph went right: he desired God above all else. We find freedom in pleasing God, not in aiming to please men. When we live to please man, we are slaves to him. When we live to please God, we are lifted from the slavery of man and brought into a beautiful honor-filled life, a life of pleasing the heart of God. The man who has made this transition can be identified simply by understanding that to be loved by God is the only approval he needs.

Questions for Reflection:

1. How often do you try to impress others for your own glorification?

2. When you live to please God, how does that affect your motives?

3. How can the truths found in this devotional be lived out in your life today?

TAKE A STAND

"His justures were of Such a personal nature I felt My self Compeled to Draw my Sword and made a signal for the boat to prepare for action at this Motion Capt. Lewis ordered all under arms in the boat, those with me also showed a Disposition to Defend themselves and me..." William Clark, September 25, 1804

The men had had enough. It was time to take a stand against the Teton Sioux. As the Sioux kept delaying the men's departure, things got out of control very quickly; tempers flared, guns were drawn, arrows were drawn and the scene was tense. Lewis and Clark decided to make a stand against the Sioux, who were unwilling to let them continue without gifts. It was a stand that very easily could have cost them their lives and ended the entire expedition.

> *"Be on alert, stand firm in the faith, act like men, be strong." 1 Corinthians 16:13*

Who will hold their ground for truth in today's world? This is what the followers of Jesus must do. We must hold our ground in a world of relativism. The world is looking for those who are willing to take a stand, even if that stand is in complete disagreement with their worldview.

At least it is a stand and recognized for what it is. Greyness has plagued the church. We must cling to the absolute truths found in Scripture. These are the things worth holding ground for, because everything that flows from our lives comes from that.

Every day, more and more Christians are compromising truth for the enemy's lies, and, in doing so, they give away tremendous ground in the battle in the heavenlies. Paul held his ground, even though it cost him everything. This is an example for us to follow.

Questions for Reflection:

1. What areas of your faith do you need to take a stand on?

2. What are the dangers of relativism?

3. How can the truths found in this devotional be lived out in your life today?

WARRIORS

"Capt clark used moderation with them told them that we must and would go on and would go. that we were not Squaws. but warriers." Sgt. John Ordway, September 25, 1804

The confrontation was tense. With guns loaded and bows drawn, the men and the Teton Sioux squared off in what would be the tensest part of the expedition. One trigger pulled or arrow let loose would have doomed the entire expedition. The men were outnumbered and would be exterminated in a short time had it come to the point of bloodshed. Lewis and Clark decided to hold their ground and fight "fire with fire" by telling the Sioux that they indeed were warriors. They wanted to make that fact clear, despite what they were up against. They demanded the respect that warriors summoned.

> *"Then Caleb quieted the people before Moses, and said, 'We should by all means go up and take possession of it, for we shall surely overcome it.'"*
> *Numbers 13:30*

Nothing is more powerful to a follower of Jesus than the identity he has been given by Christ. The world may see the Christian in all sorts of strange ways, but God sees the Christian only by one view: His.

This is the daily food that continues to nourish the soul of those who have submitted to Christ. We are warriors for righteousness; we are conquerors in Him. We are who we are because Christ says that is who we are. Our identity has nothing to do with who we think we are; it has to do with who He says we are.

This is where Caleb found his strength and courage. He viewed his life through who God said he was. God looked at Caleb and saw a man whose identity was in the promises of God. Part of the problem we face daily is that we believe the lies of the enemy, and we think we are people we are not. We must look to the people we are by realizing who Christ says we are. This is our true identity.

Questions for Reflection:

1. Are there "giants in the land" that are keeping you from obeying God's calling on your life right now?

2. Where have you looked for identity rather than in Christ?

3. How can the truths found in this devotional be lived out in your life today?

GRAND ENTRANCE

"I went on Shore on landing I was receved on a elegant painted Buffalo Robe & taken to the village by 6 men & was not permited to touch the ground untill I was put down in the grand Councill house on a White dressed Robe." William Clark, September 26, 1804

The Sioux were showing Clark great respect, and the above entry paints a scene of what would appear to be royalty and honor. Imagine Clark being carried in by six men and not being allowed to touch the ground! People knew someone important was coming to the village. What a way to enter the village!

> *"And she gave birth to her firstborn son; and she wrapped Him in cloths, and laid Him in a manger, because there was no room for them in the inn."*
> *Luke 2:7*

We have to take time to notice how Jesus entered the world, for we must do the same in the various worlds we enter in the lives of others. The Creator of the Universe chose to be born in a lowly manger. He chose to be born in a little town, to simple people.

This is the majestic beauty of the Gospel. A holy God chose to identify with lowly people, people in need of redemption. He could have chosen a marble palace, but He did not. Rather than the smells of incense and fragrance, the first aroma he smelled was that of hay and livestock manure. He chose the road of a humble servant.

In what "manger" are you birthing a new work of God? In what areas are you taking the humble road of a servant to carry the redemptive love of Christ? We identify with Jesus when we choose the "manger" over the "mansion." Everyone prefers to stay in a mansion, but Christ demands and beckons us to leave the mansion and enter the manger, for that is where He is, and that is what He did.

<u>Questions for Reflection</u>:

1. Look at your life. Would you consider yourself a "mansion" or "manger" Christian?

2. What message was Jesus sending to the world in choosing a manger to make His entrance? How should that affect the way you live?

3. How can the truths found in this devotional be lived out in your life today?

LOST ANCHOR

"Made many attempts in different ways to find our anchor, but Could not, the Sand had covered it, from the Misfortune of last night our boat was laying at shore in a verry unfavourable Situation, after finding that the anchor could not be found we deturmined to proceed on..." William Clark, September 28, 1804

The Missouri River was a constantly shifting monster of rogue currents and disappearing and reappearing sandbars. The river was very hard to navigate, and when the men stopped to trade with the Teton Sioux, the loss of their anchor was a serious problem. Without the anchor, they could not be certain that their cargo would not drift away. This would have created a huge problem. Another difficult part of the Missouri was the sandy bottom, which usually did not produce a good hold for the anchor. Occasionally the men may have anchored into a submerged log, which, although difficult to get free from, provided a certain hold in the currents.

> *"This hope we have as an anchor of the soul, a hope both sure and steadfast and one which enters within the veil." Hebrews 6:19*

The world we live in is full of unexpected turns, strange currents and unpredictable waters. Every day, we can see our lives change in drastic ways, and it is during those times that we must depend on the foundation of our faith in Jesus.

We must note that Jesus is that strong foundation that our anchor of faith can dig into and find stability and assurance. Jesus is not our anchor; our faith is. Jesus is the bedrock in which our anchor of hope and faith will hold.

The power of an anchor lies not within its size or strength, but in the stability of that into which it is being anchored. This is why the Christian can be certain in all times of life because of the "grounding" we hope in. At times, our anchor of hope and faith may be large or small. That always changes. But what never changes is who we anchor our hope and faith in ... the sure foundation of Jesus Christ.

<u>Questions for Reflection:</u>

1. What "anchors" have you placed your trust in that have proven frail and weak?

2. Knowing storms will come in life, what hope do we have in Christ being our anchor?

3. How can the truths found in this devotional be lived out in your life today?

WANT OF SLEEP

"I am veryry unwell for want of Sleep. Deturmined to Sleep to night if possible." William Clark, September 28, 1804

It is almost impossible to imagine the state Clark was in when he wrote this entry. These were men of the frontier. They were used to "roughing it." They knew hard living. They knew how to go without food, shelter or rest. But even they had breaking points.

Rest was as important to the expedition as food. If they did not rest, they could not proceed. One can almost imagine the scene as Clark wrote this entry. He was walking along, looking for that soft patch of grass with the perfect amount of cushion and foliage to keep the chilly wind away. Finding rest was not an easy thing for these men, and it must have required effort at times.

> *"Come to Me, all who are weary and heavy-laden, and I will give you rest." Matthew 11:28*

The soul of man can never be satisfied without the eternal rest found only in Jesus Christ. Man can do all possible to put on the facade of trying to find contentment, when, at the end of the day, it is rest that his soul longs for. We were created to understand this rest, and, not only to understand it, but to experience it.

This is where the unredeemed man falls short. He tells the world that he does indeed understand what it means to rest. He boasts of how certain things bring him rest. This is all the false front of a longing, unrested soul.

The saved man can be ready for death at any time because his soul has already found true rest. We long for the promise of the eternal rest we will have one day, but we also rejoice in the privilege of experiencing a fraction of that same rest at this time on earth. Our souls are at rest all the time, as they are found in the promise of God. Nothing can change that. Even if we ourselves question that rest, it is there, and we are living in it, because it is a promised rest for us now and for that glorious day when we go home to be with our King. "Come to Me!" he beckons us, for it is in Him that our rest is found, sustained and promised.

Questions for Reflection:

1. Why can true rest not be found in anything other than a relationship with Jesus Christ?

2. What does Matthew 11:28 tell you about God's heart for man?

3. How can the truths found in this devotional be lived out in your life today?

USE CAUTION

"Observe great caution this day expecting the Seaux intentions some what hostile towards our progression." William Clark, October 2, 1804

After a previous tense incident with the Sioux, the men were being cautious about any chances of further conflict. A few days prior to this entry, the men of the expedition, with guns drawn, were squared off against a vast party of Sioux warriors, with drawn bows, that vastly outnumbered them. The situation was tense, but, thankfully, it did not come to any bloodshed, and the expedition moved on cautiously through Sioux land.

> *"Behold, I send you out as sheep in the midst of wolves; therefore be shrewd as serpents, and innocent as doves." Matthew 10:16*

Jesus brings light to a few things here. The idea that He sends us out as sheep tells us a few things.

First, we need to be utterly dependent on the Shepherd. Sheep are helpless without the shepherd, just as we are helpless without Jesus in our walk in this world.

Second, sheep are kind and gentle, despite the world they live in. It is their nature. We are called to bring the gospel to a world where our message of love, grace, and forgiveness is contrary to the message the world gives.

Third, we are in the midst of the enemies of darkness. Satan and his legions of demons are out to destroy the work of God in our lives, but he is powerless if we stay close to the Shepherd.

This is why we are to use caution in our walk with Jesus. We must use caution in depending on ourselves when we need to leave our dependence on Him. We must use caution so we don't stray from bringing the true message of peace, forgiveness and grace to others. By staying close to the Shepherd and allowing Him to guide our ways, we can be cautious and keep our guard up against the schemes and traps the enemy has set for us.

Questions for Reflection:

1. How are you learning to depend on God more in your life?

2. Are you more prone to depend on yourself or others, rather than on God?

3. How can the truths found in this devotional be lived out in your life today?

WHAT IMPRESSES US

"Those Indians wer much astonished at my Servent, they never Saw a black man before, all flocked around him & examined him from top to toe." William Clark, October 10, 1804

York was the only black man in the Corps of Discovery, so it was no wonder that, when the men came into different Indian villages, the natives marveled at him. For most of them, it was the first time they had seen a black man, and they spent lots of time looking him over. It was York's physical qualities that set him apart from the other men on the expedition, and it was those physical qualities that sparked such interest among the Indians.

> *"But the Lord said to Samuel, 'Do not look at his appearance or at the height of his stature, because I have rejected him; for God sees not as man sees, for man looks at the outward appearance, but the Lord looks at the heart.'" 1 Samuel 16:7*

What is it that impresses you about certain people? If it is anything other than their sincere passion to grow in their walk with God, you need to re-align with the words spoken to Samuel.

God is not impressed by the works of man, and He asks us to see the world the way He does. If we want to be impressed by others, may it be from the observation that those people follow after Jesus. May it be that we don't see the strengths of those people, but we see Jesus in them working through their weaknesses.

When others look at us, what impresses them? Oh, what a scary question this can be, for it will often reveal how far we have drifted from Samuel's charge that the Lord gave him! May we look at ourselves and at the world with the mind of the Lord.

Questions for Reflection:

1. What is the difference between what the world is impressed by and what the Christian is impressed by?

2. What are some qualities in people that impress you and inspire you to follow hard after Jesus?

3. How can the truths found in this devotional be lived out in your life today?

DISCIPLINE...HARSH BUT NEEDED

"The punishment of this day allarmed the Indian Chief verry much, he cried aloud I explained the Cause of the punishment and the necessity of it." William Clark, October 14, 1804

One of the men of the expedition, John Newman, was court-martialed for insubordination and sentenced to 75 lashes. Lewis and Clark had to maintain stern discipline on the expedition to keep order, and, despite the harshness of the punishment, it was needed. One of the local Indian chiefs was appalled at Newman's treatment. Apparently, that tribe of Indians never laid a hand on their own children, so this form of discipline was foreign to them. Hard as it was to do, the discipline was necessary for the success of the expedition.

> *"My son, do not reject the discipline of the Lord, Or loathe His reproof, For whom the Lord loves He reproves, Even as a father, the son in whom he delights." Proverbs 3:11-12*

What we have to recognize in this Scripture is the emphasis on "For whom the Lord loves, He reproves." When God disciplines us, and He does, it is one of the most loving things He can do because He ultimately knows what is best for us.

We may *think* we know, much like a young child thinks in the bottom of his heart that a lollipop is what he needs five minutes before supper. But we have no idea what is best for us, because most of the times our motives are selfish.

We can embrace the discipline of the Lord in three stages. First is recognition that we are wrong. This is often the hardest, because it shows we have weakness. Second is accepting the discipline as a good thing for us. This has to be done willingly and with understanding. Third is learning from the discipline and changing our ways as a result of the lesson learned through the discipline. That is God's intention, that we would learn from the discipline and

37

change our behavior to become more like Him. Remember, God loves those whom He disciplines.

Questions for Reflection:

1. Which stage of embracing discipline do you struggle with the most?

2. In what areas in your life is the Lord trying to discipline you right now?

3. How can the truths found in this devotional be lived out in your life today?

COLD AND HELPLESS

"About 8 oclock PM. the thermometer fell to 74 below the freesing pointe." William Clark, December 17, 1804

As the Corps of Discovery wintered at Fort Mandan in present day North Dakota, they experienced extremely cold temperatures, colder than any of them had ever experienced before. With the weather that cold, there was not much the men could do. They could not go outside for long or they would risk severe frostbite. They spent their time mending clothing and speaking with the Mandans. These were simple things, but, all in all, they simply could not do anything but wait for the bitter cold to pass. They were helpless against the bitter Dakota winter.

> *"But God demonstrates His own love toward us, in that while we were yet sinners, Christ died for us."*
> Romans 5:8

One of the greatest revelations man can have is that he can do nothing to merit God's love. God's love is not earned; it is simply given. When man realizes he is completely helpless without God, it is there he finds life.

Of all the gifts in the world, none could be more beautiful than the gift of being accepted as we are, no strings attached. Of all the gifts in the world, none could be as loving as being unconditionally loved while we are filled with selfish sin. Of all the gifts in the world, none could be as life changing as the truth that we can never do anything to *make* God love us.

He loves us because of who He is, not because of who we are. We are helpless without the love of God, and this is a beautiful place to be because it points us to the foot of the cross, stained with the blood of the Savior who came to us while we were His enemies and helpless. What a glorious revelation of divine love!

Questions for Reflection:

1. How does the fact that Jesus came to us while we were helpless transform the way you live?

2. How does this truth compare to other world religions?

3. How can the truths found in this devotional be lived out in your life today?

ONE BUFFALO ROBE

"The Indians of the lower Village turned out to hunt for a man & a boy who had not returned from the hunt yesterday, and borrow'd a Slay to bring them in excpecting to find them frosed to death about 10 oClocok the boy about 13 years of age Came to the fort with his feet frosed and had layed out last night without fire with only a Buffalow Robe to Cover him...Customs & the habots of those people has anured them to bare more Cold than I thought it possible for man to endure." William Clark, January 10, 1805

One of the most amazing things about the Lewis and Clark expedition was the shear rawness of nature. Probably one of the hardest times for them was their first winter, which was spent in present day North Dakota with the Mandan Indians. Temperatures dropped to as low as -40. Often, the men never left the rough-cut cabins they had built because it was so cold. It was in this bitter cold that we see an amazing attribute to the Mandan Indians, how they over time had adapted to the harsh conditions on the northern plains. The cold did not seem to affect them nearly as much as it did the white men.

> *"Trust in the Lord, and lean not on your own understanding." Proverbs 3:5*

It is hard to even imagine how a person could survive in such harsh weather with one buffalo robe. It is interesting that the search party went out with a sled, as they expected the boy to be dead. We can imagine the utter shock on the men's faces as that 13-year-old strolled into camp alive! Impossible!

How many times in our lives have we thought the same of the faithfulness of God? We look at the blizzards of life, and we say, "No way, God! There is no way we can survive this!" When we think about it, we need to wonder if that 13-year-old Mandan lad had more faith in a buffalo robe to save his life than we do in Jesus to save us from life's trials.

Oh, that we would trust Him in His promise of faithfulness! If we lean on our own understanding, where then do we learn to trust in Christ? "Trust Me!" is what the Savior commands. We need not try to understand the blizzard, but to trust that the "robe" He provides will be sufficient to get us through.

Questions for Reflection:

1. Do you find it easy to focus on the "blizzards" rather than the faithfulness of God?

2. What can you do to begin to trust God more in the midst of trials?

3. How can the truths found in this devotional be lived out in your life today?

ICE COLD

"All hands employed in cutting the Perogues Loose from the ice, which was nearly even with their top; we found great dificuelty in effecting this work owing to the different devisiosn of Ice & water." William Clark, February 23, 1805

As the men stayed at Fort Mandan for the winter, their pirogues (small canoes) became enveloped in ice, almost up to the top. So, as the weather warmed a bit, they used the opportunities to chip away the countless layers of ice that had built up over the cold winter. It was a hard process that took time and hard work. The ice had literally encased the pirogues, making the work extremely difficult.

> *"But Jesus on his part, was not entrusting Himself to them, for he knew all men." John 2:24*

Jesus did not trust the crowds that often followed Him, because their hearts had grown cold. This is a warning to us all to know that our hearts can grow so cold that Jesus walks by us, knowing that our cold hearts are incapable of melting due to their hardness.

Hearts do not grow cold in an instant; it is a lengthy process that builds layer upon layer, until we leave no room for Christ to melt those layers. This is why we need to confess of our sins daily, constantly asking the Holy Spirit to melt the ice layers on our hearts. When we allow Him to melt our hearts daily, the ice of sin cannot take hold, for it has no power. But when we treat our sin lightly, merely brushing it off without going to the cross, it is then that the layers slowly but surely build on each other, until the core of the heart is no longer accessible.

<u>Questions for Reflection:</u>

1. How lightly do you take certain sins?

2. What danger do you face by not confessing your sins daily to God?

3. How can the truths found in this devotional be lived out in your life today?

CAREFUL PLACEMENT

"I observed extrodanary dexterity of the indians in jumping from one cake of ice to another, for the purpose of Cathcing the buffalowas they float down many of the cakes of ice which they pass over are not two feet square." William Clark, March 30, 1805

The above scene is amazing. In freezing cold rivers, the Mandan Indians would jump from one block of ice to another to catch dead drifting buffalo. The risk was tremendous. We can imagine that there were times when this technique went sour, and men perished in the frigid waters of the Missouri. The Indians had to be extremely accurate when they placed themselves on those blocks of ice.

> *"Abram settled in the land of Canaan, while Lot settled in the cities of the valley and moved his tents as far as Sodom; now the men of Sodom were wicked exceedingly and sinners against the Lord." Genesis 13:12-13*

We must be careful where we place ourselves; this is the lesson of Lot's life. Deep within his heart, Lot knew that setting up camp near Sodom would lead to his demise. But he let the flesh control him.

Where are we placing ourselves on a day-to-day basis? The answer will show us whether we are growing closer to Jesus or farther from Him.

We all have weaknesses that we are aware of, and each day those lands of weakness cry out to us to come to them. We cannot. When we do, the result will always be the same.

At times, God brings us to a place we think will get us in trouble, because we know that area may be a weakness. But the difference is it is His leading, not our own. His leading always has truth and sanctification in mind; our leading always has self in mind. His leading, where He places us in life, is always on sure stable ground. And it is that ground we must stand on.

45

Questions for Reflection:

1. Do your daily decisions and actions place you closer to Jesus or farther from Him?

2. In what ways can you become more careful about where you position your thoughts, motives and actions?

3. How can the truths found in this devotional be lived out in your life today?

GRAVELINE SAVES THE DAY

"Mr. Gravlin who speaks the Ricara language extremely well, has been employed to conduct a few of the Recara chiefs to the seat of government who promised us to decend in the barge." Meriwhether Lewis, April 7, 1805

In the fall of 1804, the Lewis and Clark expedition entered what is present-day North Dakota. In this land they were entering unfamiliar terrain, a land full of tribes about whom they had heard many negative rumors. In the vastness of that amazing expedition was a man about whom history seldom speaks, a man named Joseph Graveline. Graveline had been living with the Arikara Indians for 13 years. He knew the country, and he spoke Sioux, French, English and Arikara. He played a vital role in communicating among the tribes and the Corps of Discovery. Clear communication was hard to come by with all the different languages, so his role was a huge help to the expedition.

> *"My sheep hear My voice, and I know them, and they follow me." John 10:27*

Not much has changed when it comes to problems we have with others. Often the problems we have had with people have been the result of exactly what was hurting the diplomacy with the Sioux: bad communication.

And while we are at it, most of the problems we have with our relationship with Jesus have to do with bad communication, all on our part. Why is it that we make our communicating with Jesus such a theological, intellectual matter? Why is it that we doubt He is constantly wanting to properly communicate His truth to us?

Oh, that we would believe that God speaks to us, and He is more concerned about properly communicating with us than we are about communicating with Him! Oh that we could trust His words, stop doubting whether or not He is communicating with us, and begin to take hold of the beautiful truth that He does...and is...and always will be! The "translation" of His love through the life, death, and resurrection of His Son is never faulty; it can always be trusted.

Questions for Reflection:

1. In what ways do you communicate with God?

2. In what ways do you find yourself doubting that God has spoken to you?

3. How can the truths found in this devotional be lived out in your life today?

THE HAPPIEST DAY

"We were now about to penetrate a country at least two thousand miles in width, on which the foot of civilized man had never trodden; the good or evil it had in store for us was for experiment yet to determin...I could but esteem this moment of my departure as among the most happy of my life." Meriwhether Lewis, April 7, 1805

Lewis wrote this entry in his journal after the long hard winter in the Mandan village, as they were departing to go into a completely uncharted mass of land acquired from the Louisiana Purchase. It was an exciting time, and Lewis's words show us his relishing of that great day of unexpected adventure! That day when, with one step, he was beginning a journey into the unknown.

> *"By faith Abraham, when he was called, obeyed by going out to a place which he was to receive for an inheritance; and he went out, not knowing where he was going." Hebrews 11:8*

Something kindles the fire of the soul when we take leaps of faith into the unknown, utterly dependent upon Jesus for every need. It is those times in our faith journey when we look with anticipation at the future, not knowing at all what it entails, but certain in moving forward because we have heard from the Lord to do so.

These days are some of the happiest of our lives because we throw our own cautious calculations out the window and jump into reckless abandonment with Jesus! Jesus loves it when we look into the uncertain future, jump into His arms and say, "Let's go! I don't have it all figured out, but I trust in you!" By this, we put a smile on the Savior's face! When we make Jesus smile, those are the happiest days we could have.

These are the days when we, by our reckless faith, declare to Him that He is in control of our lives, and we trust His sovereign hand to lead us in His path. Abraham heard from God and obeyed...despite the uncertainty of his future. This is key for us to

49

remember, that it happened in that order...he first heard from the Lord; then he went. May the voice of the Lord always be the beginning step in our next adventures into the unknown!

Questions for Reflection:

1. Is God asking you to take a step of faith in a certain area of your life?

2. When was the last time you took a risk for God?

3. How can the truths found in this devotional be lived out in your life today?

BEHIND THE SCENES

"When we halted for dinner the squaw busied herself in serching for the wild artichokes which the mice collect and deposit in large hoards." Meriwhether Lewis, April 9, 1805

The expedition could never have succeeded without Sacajawea. She proved an extremely important member of the Corps of Discovery, not to mention the fact that she literally raised a newborn baby along the way. She had an immense knowledge of the land and would often do many behind-the-scenes tasks that contributed tremendously to the welfare of the expedition. She was always gathering native herbs and roots to use for food or medicinal purposes, as well as recognizing landmarks to help guide the way. Her skills, though often behind the scenes, were essential to the expedition's success.

> *"And since we have gifts that differ according to the grace given to us, let each exercise them accordingly..."Romans 12:6*

When we live our lives for an audience of One, we have accomplished all we are to do while here on earth. If the world were a stage and our audience were the person Jesus Christ, how would we live? The deeds we perform should always be birthed out of a sincere desire to please Him. It is out of this desire that a genuine desire to serve man will come.

The true follower of Jesus does not relish in the glory bestowed upon him by man, because it is that glory that takes the focus away from Jesus and puts it on ourselves. May this never be!

When we live for an audience of One, everything we do is an act of worship; everything we do has sacred value; everything we do has eternal consequences; and everything we do is a reflection of our devotion to Him. Let us live our lives in a way that provides contentment with "behind-the-scenes" tasks, for that phrase is man-made. There is no such thing as "behind-the-scenes" ministry with Jesus, for everything is before His eyes, and nothing takes precedence over anything else. All is an act of worship to Him.

Questions of Reflection:

1. What would your life look like if you embraced living for an audience of One?

2. In what ways do you struggle to "be known" and recognized by others?

3. How can the truths found in this devotional be lived out in your life today?

GENTLE CURIOUSITY

"The buffaloe Elk and Antelope are so gentle that we pass near them while feeding, without appearing to excite any alarm among them; and when we attract their attention, they frequently approach us more nearly to discover what we are." Meriwhether Lewis, April 25, 1805

In today's world, it is almost impossible to imagine the above description of wildlife. Due to the lack of their interaction with men, the wildlife had no fear of them. In fact, it appears that many times the animals were more curious about the men than frightened by them.

> *"Then Jerusalem was going out to him, and all Judea, and all the district around Jordan; and they were being baptized by him in the Jordan River, as they confessed their sins." Matthew 3:5-6*

What is it about you that makes others curious about Jesus? When you meet people who have had all sorts of "experiences" with the church and Christians, but who have never had a genuine experience with Jesus, how do you appear to them?

Something about John the Baptist made others come to him out of curiosity. When it comes to Jesus, many people are like the wildlife in our forests. When they see Christians, they simply run the other way because of past experiences, prejudices, etc. But some are curious about why we follow Jesus. These are the people we must reach with the Gospel of love and peace! What are we doing that makes them curious about the Jesus they see in us?

Questions for Reflection:

1. Does your life draw others to be curious about the Gospel?

2. What do you think it was about John the Baptist that drew the crowds?

3. How can the truths found in this devotional be lived out in your life today?

SIMPLE PLEASURES

"In order to add in some measure to the general pleasure which seemed to pervade our little community, we ordered a dram to be issued to each person; this soon produced the fiddle, and they spent the evening with much hilarity, singing and dancing, and seemed as perfectly to forget their past toils, as they appeared regardless of those to come." Meriwhether Lewis, April 26, 1805

One of the most amazing feats of the whole expedition was the extremely small number of inter-personal problems that rose up in the Corps of Discovery. After the crew left the Mandan Villages, they were in high spirits, and Lewis and Clark hardly ever had to deal with insubordination. This entry from Lewis' journal gives a glimpse into the atmosphere of the men after their long hard winter on the plains of North Dakota, as they arrived at the fork of the Missouri and Yellowstone Rivers.

Lewis and Clark knew that in order to get the optimum performance from the men, they had to allow the simple pleasures in life. They had to let the guys take a breather, laugh and enjoy the things that brought cheer to their hearts. This was a priceless gift they gave their men.

"Delight yourself in the Lord; and He will give you the desires of your heart." Psalm 37:4

We need to be grateful that Jesus does the same for us. Living the Christian life is tough and can be extremely taxing. Maybe one of the reasons Jesus was ridiculed for being a drunkard was that He took time to hang with the guys over a goblet of wine. He took simple pleasure in the sweet taste, but, more than that, He connected with the people. His disciples were risking their lives following Him, and He knew it was tough on them. He allowed them the time to enjoy simple things, like a goblet of wine.

Jesus cares for those simple things that bring us joy. Jesus knows what those simple desires of our heart are, whether it be a hot cup of coffee, a phone call from a friend, or simply the ability to rest, and He willingly loves to give us those simple blessings, for they help us stay sane in a crazy world.

Questions for Reflection:

1. What are some of the simple pleasures you have that you can thank God for today?

2. Think about some of the desires of your heart. Have you committed them to God?

3. How can the truths found in this devotional be lived out in your life today?

LOOK AROUND YOU

"Game is still very abundant we can scarcely cast our eyes in any direction without percieving deer Elk Buffaloe or Antelopes." Meriwhether Lewis, April 29, 1805

Imagine the scene: trudging along in modern day Montana, looking out and seeing wildlife everywhere. Wildlife was so abundant that the men, during this particular time, had only to look up to see elk, buffalo and other animals all around them. There was no need to search for the animals; they were everywhere. It was a scene so grand that it is almost impossible to imagine.

> *"Oh the glorious splendor of Thy majesty, And on Thy wonderful works, I will meditate." Psalm 145:5*

The follower of Jesus sees God at work everywhere, in all places, at all times. Through thick and thin, we do not need to search for the works of God. He is always working, and His will is being played out in the lives of those who follow Him.

When was the last time you found yourself trying to find God moving in your life? Do not search; instead recognize and accept the fact that He is working. That is the life of reckless faith. Though we do not see, we know.

The Holy Spirit works in ways we often do not see or understand, but that does not change the fact that He is working all the time. "Proof! I want proof!" cries the skeptic, while at the same time breaths of oxygen are bringing life to his lungs, but he cannot see it.

Train yourself to see the works of God around you, and you *will* see them. Ask God to show His continual work in the lives of those around you, and you will.

Questions for Reflection:

1. When was the last time you stopped and looked around at the beauty of God's creation and worshiped Him for it?

2. Where is God working in your life that you may have taken for granted or simply been too busy to recognize?

3. How can the truths found in this devotional be lived out in your life today?

UNDERESTIMATED FOE

"The Indians may well fear this anamal equipped as they generally are with their bows and arrows or indifferent fuzees, but in the hands of skillfull riflemen they are by no means as formidable or dangerous as they have been respresented. I find that the curiosity of our party is pretty well satisfyed with rispect to this anamal." *Meriwhether Lewis, April 29, 1805*

As the expedition began to move along the Yellowstone River, they were eager for their first encounter with a "Yellow Bear," which today we would call the grizzly. The journals reveal a very insightful look into how Lewis first underestimated the fierceness of the grizzly. Although he gave credit to the grizzly for its huge size and ability to survive multiple shots from slugs, Lewis still said that a "skilled hunter" (as if the Indians were not skilled hunters!) with a rifle could easily take down a grizzly. Later on, after multiple encounters with the savage beast, Lewis's journals show he had a change of mind. After a few near death experiences with grizzlies, some of which required up to six men and eight slugs to bring down a grizzly, Lewis probably realized he had underestimated the strength of that foe. His underestimation almost cost his life and the lives of others.

> *"For if anyone thinks he is something when he is nothing, he deceives himself."* Galatians 6:3

I wonder how many times we underestimate the powers of darkness. How many times in our lives have we been prideful, thinking we could conquer anything, only to fall flat on our faces?

We have complete victory in Christ, but we need not underestimate the degree to which Satan and his legions of demons hate us and want to destroy us. Even more than that, we cannot underestimate our frailty and laziness. We cannot fall into a lazy spiritual slumber, for when we do, our guard goes down.

Let us be careful not to underestimate the enemy of our souls, nor to overestimate the pride that may overtake us in moments of self-glorification. These times will always rise up as we walk with

59

Jesus, but, when they do, we can get rid of our pride and rely on His grace to see us through.

Questions for Reflection:

1. In what ways have you underestimated your own weakness of the flesh?

2. How can you live a life of walking in your identity in Christ while at the same time not underestimating the reality of Satan and his power?

3. How can the truths found in this devotional be lived out in your life today?

KEEP YOUR COOL

"Charbono still crying to his god for mercy, had not yet recollected the rudder, nor could the repeated orders of the Bowsman, Cruzat, bring him to his recollection untill he threatened to shoot him instantly if he did not take hold of the rudder and do his duty." Meriwhether Lewis, May 14, 1805

We all have our good traits and our not-so-good ones. Sometimes the good ones show; other times the bad.

Toussaint Charbonneau was an invaluable part of the Corps of Discovery. Not only did he introduce Lewis and Clark to one of his Indian wives, Sacajawea, who history shows was a cornerstone in their success, but he served as an interpreter, which also proved to be invaluable.

Charbonneau had his good traits, but he also had his bad ones. Perhaps one of his biggest faults came to light at a most perilous time in the expedition. While traveling on the Missouri River, a squall kicked up and the pirogue he was in began to sink. It was an extremely dangerous situation for a number of reasons. The first was that Charbonneau himself, along with others, could not swim. The second was that Sacajawea was on the pirogue with her baby, and they were about 300 yards from shore. The third was that much valuable cargo, including Lewis' journals, began to float away.

To the surprise of many, Charbonneau buckled under the situation. Under pressure, he did not keep a cool head. He allowed the fear of uncertainty to cloud his judgment. He buckled, and it almost cost the lives of others, had not some intervened.

> *"But you, be sober in all things, endure hardship, do the work of an evangelist, fulfill your ministry."* 2 Timothy 4:5

Walking with Jesus is an amazing journey. For all the amazing things our journey with Him brings, it also brings many difficult times and trials. They come in all shapes, sizes, and fashions.

The question we must ask ourselves is not *if* they come, because we know they will, but *how* will we respond to the tough times when they do come. When all seems out of control, when it appears as if our boat is sinking, how do we respond? In other words, we need to hold our ground. We need to stay level headed and not buckle under the pressures of life.

When we try to bear hardships on our own, we will fail. We must submit them to the Father, for His shoulders are broad. To be sober in all things demands that we keep our cool, think things through, assess the times we are going through, and hold our ground based on Jesus' promise.

When He tells us He will never leave us or forsake us, and He never gives us more than we can handle. We need to embrace His control during the seemingly catastrophic times in life.

Questions for Reflection:

1. How do you usually respond during difficult times and trials?

2. What promises does Jesus have for you to help during difficult times?

3. How can the truths found in this devotional be lived out in your life today?

UNDERESTIMATED FOE

"But when I reflected on the difficulties which this snowey barrier would most probably throw my way to the Pacific, and the sufferings and hardships of myself and party in thim, it in some measurements counterbalanced the joy I had felt in the first moments in which I gazed upon them." Meriwhether Lewis, May 26, 1805

Lewis' heart was filled with awe and excitement as he gazed upon the Rocky Mountains. He pondered their beauty, their majesty, their awesomeness. At the same time, that same awesomeness brought reality quickly, as he saw the snow-capped peaks and imagined the hard times that were to come as they traveled through them.

> *"But if anyone suffers as a Christian, let him not feel ashamed, but in that name let him glorify God."*
> *1 Peter 4:16*

When we first come to Jesus, we are faced with looking at pure beauty and enchantment. We have been redeemed, rescued, forgiven and justified. We cannot help but rejoice and tell others of the amazing rebirth we have had.

Then life happens, and we begin to realize that the Christian walk is not for the faint of heart. In fact, nothing is more difficult. This life is actually so difficult that it is impossible for us to live the Christian life on our own, but this is where Jesus steps in and says, "It's okay. I did not intend for you to live the perfect life. That's why I came to this earth."

Following Jesus has a tremendous cost. In our pillow-softened Christianity, we often do not realize this, because our faith has cost us nothing. Then the day comes when we experience a sense of persecution for bearing the name of Jesus, and we stand in shock, as if we did not expect hardships. But we must realize that hardships are part of walking with Jesus. After all, He took the road of loneliness, hardship, and shame to provide our salvation. If He willingly embraced that road, should we not also?

Questions for Reflection:

1. How is your perspective on suffering and persecution?

2. What does Jesus teach you about enduring shame, scorn and persecution?

3. How can the truths found in this devotional be lived out in your life today?

FOLLOW WISELY

"Today we passed on the Stard. side the remains of a vast many mangled carcases of Buffalow which had benn driven over a precipice of 120 feet by the indians and perished." Meriwhether Lewis, May 29, 1805

This entry explains the results of a classic technique the Indians would use to kill buffalo. They would have men dress up as buffalo, get as close to the herd as possible and have others startle the buffalo. The lead man would run, and, naturally, the other buffalo would follow to their deaths as the individual would jump under a small over-hang and hold on while hundreds of buffalo would jump over the cliff crushing each other. The key was getting the buffalo to follow the lead decoy. Following that person led to their deaths.

> *"And Jesus said to them, 'Follow Me, and I will make you fishers of men.'" Mark 1:17*

It is worthy to note that Jesus commanded Simon and Andrew to follow Him. It was not a suggestion or a question of "Will you follow me?" Rather, it was a command given to be obeyed.

It is crucial to understand that we become that which we follow. Or, more importantly, we become *whom* we follow. Jesus gave this command to follow Him, because He knows the "God path" for our lives. He is the one who knows what lies ahead. So when we follow Him, whether in good times or bad, we are on the right path because He is leading us.

Man will always fail when he follows man. This is what happened to Adam and Eve: they followed each other rather than the command of the Lord. This is what happened to Lot's wife: she followed her own curiosity rather than the command of the Lord. This is what happened to Judas when he betrayed Jesus: he followed the temptations of the flesh.

Following anyone except the Lord will result in death, all the time. Following what or whom you want to follow may seem okay at the time, but it eventually will crumble, for nothing lasts except that which comes from Him. Following Jesus takes a daily decision of submissive obedience to a Sovereign plan determined by a personal God, planned for our daily sanctification.

Questions for Reflection:

1. What lessons can you learn from the examples of Lot, Judas, and Adam and Eve when it comes to following people rather than God?

2. How are you when it comes to following God's plan, as opposed to your own?

3. How can the truths found in this devotional be lived out in your life today?

INTERRUPTIONS

"Last night we were allarmed by a large buffaloe Bull, which swam over from the opposite shore and coming along side of the white perogue, climbed over it to land, he then allarmed ran up the bank in full speed directly towards the fires, and was within 18 inches of the heads of some of the men who lay sleeping." Meriwhether Lewis, May 29, 1805

This was a close call. The raging buffalo almost killed some of the men who were sleeping, as it trampled on some of the men's things, including York's gun. The men were enjoying a night's sleep; they were comfortable and relaxed, when all of a sudden this buffalo interrupted their evening in classic fashion. It must have been a sight to see and something the men would remember every time they laid their heads down to rest.

> *"So Abram went forth as the Lord had spoken to him..." Genesis 12:4a*

How willing are you to allow God to interrupt your life when all seems normal? When things are going according to your plans, and when you are used to the comfort of everyday life, are you open to allowing God to rush in out of nowhere and destroy your plans and replace them with *His* plans?

Oh, the question of obedience! Abram gave God the permission to interrupt his life, and it was because of that step of faith that Abram was then taken on the most tremendous adventure of his life. But it had to start with Abram being open for an interrupted life. When it comes to allowing God to guide us, He would rather see his people as flowers he can pick and move on his command than as rooted oak trees, set in our ways and refusing to budge.

Questions for Reflection:

1. What does it mean to allow God to interrupt your life?

2. Are you a flower easily removed and replanted or an oak that is set in your ways and plans?

3. How can the truths found in this devotional be lived out in your life today?

WITHOUT A MURMUR

"In short their labour is incredibly painfull and great, yet those faithfull fellows bear it without a murmur." Meriwhether Lewis, May 31, 1805

Although important, it was not the planning of the expedition that made it successful. It was not the food that sustained the men that made it successful. It was not the fact that the majority of the tribes were friendly to them that made it successful. It was not the leadership of Lewis and Clark that made it successful. All of these attributed to the success, of course, but probably the biggest reason for the success of the Lewis and Clark expedition was simply the inspiring attitudes of the men to push on. It was their attitudes that made the expedition succeed.

> *"Do all things without grumbling or disputing, that you may prove yourselves to be blameless and innocent, children of God above reproach." Philippians 2:15*

Satan has many schemes to destroy a Christian's walk. However, of all the tactics he uses, probably the most effective is when he steps aside and allows Christians to destroy their own lives by their own attitudes. Complaining is one of those attitudes that can quickly destroy the work of God in the life of a believer.

When things get tough, it is so easy for us to complain, because that allows us to focus on blaming others for what is actually an issue in our own hearts. When we complain, we also take the focus off of Christ and put in on the situation we are complaining about, which only leads to more frustration and complaining.

If anyone in the world had reason to complain, it was Jesus; yet He muttered not one word of complaint while on earth. That is amazing when you think of all the situations He could have complained about. Complaining is another rotten fruit that shows our unbelieving attitude that Christ is not sufficient for every situation we find ourselves in. Complaining reveals a lack of complete trust in Him.

Questions for Reflection:

1. Are there any areas that you tend to complain about?

2. Why would complaining hinder the depth of your trust in God?

3. How can the truths found in this devotional be lived out in your life today?

TOUGH BUT RIGHT DECISION

"Those ideas as they occured to me I indevoured to impress on the minds of the party all of whom exceopt Capt. C. being still firm in the belief that the N.Fork was the Missouri and that which we ought to take." Meriwhether Lewis, June, 1805

It was an extremely tough decision; the future of the entire expedition rested on whether Lewis and Clark made the right call. In what is now present day Montana, they had come to an unexpected fork in the Missouri. They had to figure out which fork was the right one. To make the wrong call meant logistical, political and emotional disaster. At the end of numerous conversations and scouting trips, Lewis and Clark decided to take the southern route, as opposed to the more popular northern one. As a matter of fact, Lewis and Clark were the only ones on the expedition who believed the southern route was the right one. Despite the overwhelming odds of the group's consensus, they stuck to their decision, and history reveals that it was the correct one.

> *"But if any of you lack wisdom, let him ask of God, who gives to all men generously and without reproach, and it will be given him." James 1:5*

What is it that guides our decisions? Where do we derive wisdom from? More importantly, when the pressure comes from others, do our decisions lie within the parameters of Scripture and the mind of Christ? Do we make decisions as the Bible would counsel us to?

I see from the above story four scriptural guidelines for decision making. The first is to consult others whom you know have Godly wisdom. Second, don't rush into important decisions. Instead, take your time, think through things and seek the Lord. If these men had rushed things, the whole expedition would have faltered! Third, sometimes you just have to go with your gut.

At times the Holy Spirit gives us these "gut feelings" for a reason, and usually He is the best at helping us know what to do. Fourth, do your research; count the cost; check the signs. Lewis and

Clark ended up making the decision for the southern route based on two main things: the color of the water and the shape of the stones within. They had to study and look them over.

When faced with big decisions, we need to do our homework within these four scriptural parameters. Wisdom is a gift of God and a gift that the Scriptures say He gives liberally, so we can expect to receive wisdom and walk in thankfulness.

Questions for Reflection:

1. How many of your decisions are made within the parameters of biblical thought?

2. In what ways do you need to grow in wisdom about decision making?

3. How can the truths found in this devotional be lived out in your life today?

STAYING BUSY

"Those who have remained at camp today have been busily engaged in dressing skins for clothing, notwithstanding that many of them have their feet so mangled and bruised with the stones and rough ground over which they passed barefoot, that they can scarcely walk or stand." Meriwether Lewis, June 3, 1805

The men of the expedition did not have much time to lie around and be lazy. They had to stay busy with the everyday things that were essential for their survival. If they slacked off, they perished -- plain and simple. Whether it was hunting, repairing things, cleaning skins, etc., they kept busy with the essential tasks needed to make the expedition succeed. They had to; their lives depended on it.

> *"Go to the ant, O sluggard, Observe her ways and be wise, Which, having no chief, Officer or ruler, Prepares her food in the summer, And gathers her provision in the harvest." Proverbs 6:6*

Give a man too much down time without focus and inevitably that will lead to failure. If King David himself fell into a terrible pattern of sin due to laziness and bad time management, do we not think it could happen to us?

Everything is a gift from God and must be honored and treated accordingly, including what we do with our time. The proverb above eludes to working and what happens when we don't work. But a more important lesson we see here is that our spirits must be exercised and managed as well. For if we get lazy, spiritually speaking, the end result is not good.

We fail, time and time again. Jesus asks us to be about His Father's business. That is what we must do with our time, whether it be in study, fellowship, worship, service, even in our hobbies. We have to keep the razor of time management sharp with the Spirit of God. We have to keep busy with the heavenly things, for that is where we are sanctified more and more into the likeness of Christ.

We must stay busy with the heavenly things. We have to do that as though our lives depended on it.

Questions for Reflection:

1. Would you consider yourself a good manager of your time in terms of being about the Father's business?

2. Are there any areas in your life where you are becoming "spiritually lazy"?

3. How can the truths found in this devotional be lived out in your life today?

WITHOUT A MURMUR

"I now laid myself down on some willow boughs to a comfortable nights rest, and felt indeed as if I was fully repaid for the toil and pain of the day, so muchwill a good shelter, a dry bed, and comfortable supper revive the sperits of the waryed, wet and hungry traveler." Meriwhether Lewis, June 7, 1805

Often it is the simplest things in life that mean the most and bring the most joy. As the Lewis and Clark expedition trudged on day after day, the utter exhaustion the men felt was at times unbearable. Fatigue, hunger, soreness, lack of sleep, the constant irritation of the elements and pestering mosquitoes were everyday realities. Lewis and Clark knew the men needed a break every now and then, and it was the simple things that provided so much encouragement.

> *"Every good thing bestowed and every perfect gift is from above, coming down from the Father of lights."*
> *James 1:17*

We live in such a fast paced world that we often do not realize the gifts of God that we are privileged to receive every day: a warm bed, a hot cup of coffee on a cold morning, a warm shower, and food in our bellies.

It is usually the times when we lack the simplest things that cause us to appreciate them. This should not be. Every pleasure we enjoy screams forth, "To God be praised and to Him be the glory!" For He is the source of all our contentment and blessings.

What a reminder of the act of worship that is required of us when we receive the gifts we have, whatever they may be. From the simplest gifts, like the warm sun on our skin, to the most awe inspiring gift of eternal life through Jesus Christ, may we always remember to ponder on such things and turn that pondering into worship of the Great Giftgiver.

Questions for Reflection:

1. Take time to list some simple things in life that you take for granted.

2. How can a cup of coffee be an opportunity to worship Jesus?

3. How can the truths found in this devotional be lived out in your life today?

PRESSING ON

"We all believe that we are about to enter on the most perilous and dificuelt part of our Voyage, yet I see no one repineing; all appear ready to meet those difficulties which await us with resolution and becomeing fortitude." William Clark, June 20, 1805

Clark wrote this in his journal just before they were about to attempt the great 18-mile portage around the Great Falls of the Missouri. The men of the expedition were realists; they knew the trials that were ahead. Although they had no idea in what form they would come, they all recognized the reality that those trials would indeed come. This expedition was no walk in the park; it was a daily battle between life and death in many ways, yet the men met the difficulties and trials with grit, determination and admirable perseverance.

> *"Blessed are those who have been persecuted for the sake of righteousness, for theirs is the kingdom of heaven. Blessed are you when men cast insults at you, and persecute you, and say all kinds of evil against you falsely, on account of Me. Rejoice and be glad, for your reward in heaven is great..." Matthew 5:10-12*

The word we must grasp here is "blessed." This is what our Savior wants us to realize. He asks us to see two things in the face of persecution and scorn that the world with throw our way: the kingdom of heaven and our reward in heaven.

The kingdom belongs to us when we are persecuted. What a privilege to be given a kingdom for the sake of Christ! The reward we shall receive is a heavenly one, and this is good because it is the heavenly rewards that truly last. The kingdom of heaven and the rewards of heaven are the heavenly currency we shall inherit every time we are scorned for the sake of the Gospel.

"On account of Me," our Savior says. This is why we shall with joy receive scorn, insults and persecution. How blessed we are on account of Him, to be faced with trials in the present, but with the promises of eternal blessings in the future.

Questions for Reflection:

1. What is the biblical definition of "being blessed"? How does that definition differ from the way you may have viewed it in the past?

2. What does the promise that persecution will come make you realize about following Jesus?

3. How can the truths found in this devotional be lived out in your life today?

STAKES IN THE PRAIRIE

"I direct stakes to be cut to stick up in the praries to show the way for the party to transport the baggage." William Clark, June 20, 1805

Most of the men of the expedition were raised in the woods. Being from the Eastern woodlands, the men had grown accustomed to navigating through the deep forests, using trees, ridges, meadows, and mountain peaks as guiding compasses to direct their paths. With trees all around them for most of their lives, it must have been a shock to stumble upon the vast grasslands of the Great Plains.

So when they came to a landscape that had none of those things they were familiar with, they must have been concerned. It was time for them to get creative and learn a new way to navigate through the vast grasslands. By placing sticks in the ground at intervals, Clark engineered a way to guide the men. Then they had something to show them the way.

> *"Thy Word is a lamp unto my feet, and a light to my path." Psalm 119:105*

Life can represent the vast grasslands of uncertainty at times. In a world where everything is "okay," it can become more and more difficult to "find your way" in life. Unfortunately, we Christians also get overwhelmed at all the things in this world, and sometimes we become lost in our walk with Jesus.

But all along, the Lord has made it as simple and as ingenious as a stake on the prairie for us to find our way. How is that? By staying close to His Word. It is His Word--that is the one true ultimate guide we have to navigate through any terrain life takes us. Our emotions will fail us, our friends will disappoint us, and our wills will often mislead us, but God's Word never falters...ever.

There is no magic formula, no shortcut. We simply must stay in His Word, saturate ourselves in it, and on the horizon we will always see that next stake of guidance He has in the ground of our hearts for us.

Questions for Reflection:

1. In what ways does the world specifically try to disorient you from your walk with Jesus?

2. How can you daily navigate through the "grasslands of life" without getting lost?

3. How can the truths found in this devotional be lived out in your life today?

FROM LEADER TO COOK

"...for myself I continued to act the part of the cook in order to keep all hands employed." Meriwhether Lewis, June 26, 1805

One of the extraordinary feats that Lewis and Clark accomplished during the expedition was that they earned the utmost respect from all the men of the Corps of Discovery. It is worthy to note that even though the expedition was a military one, Lewis and Clark earned respect from the men not by lording rank over them, but by serving them and leading by example.

Although it was a military expedition, and they occasionally did have to use rank to keep things in line, they primarily served their men. During the time of the great 18-mile portage around the Great Falls of the Missouri, an amazing amount of hard work needed to be done, and, given the fact that their group was small, everyone had to help out, no matter their rank.

And this is where, in one of his journal entries, Lewis shines his brightest. Here we see a great example of a true leader. Lewis "stooped" to the simple task of being a cook for his men. He did not think himself too good for that task. The men needed food, and he was going to be the one to make it. Here he showed great servanthood and humility.

> *"Have this attitude in yourselves which was also in Christ Jesus, who, although He existed in the form of God, did not regard equality with God a thing to be grasped, but emptied Himself, taking the form of a bond-servant, and being made in the likeness of men." Philippians 2:5-7*

The follower of Jesus should shudder in awe when he ponders the humility of Jesus Christ, who was the perfect example of humility. What an amazing, humble, loving Savior, a Savior who does not "Lord it" over us, in spite of the fact that He is the Creator of everything in this world.

Rather, we are reminded that He humbly took our place on the cross and died a death we deserved. Jesus became the sin of the world to redeem mankind. He deserves our admiration and respect, our highest devotion. Serving Jesus comes from the utmost respect of Him becoming lesser, so we could become greater. This is what the cross reminds us of. May we look at our lives through the humble lens of the cross. From King to servant--He came for us.

Questions for Reflection:

1. How often do you find yourself taking the role of a servant leader?

2. How should the humility of Christ transform you?

3. How can the truths found in this devotional be lived out in your life today?

PERFECTLY DESIGNED

"And from which had they made one false step they must have been precipitated at least a 500 feet. this anamal appears to frequent such precepices and clifts where in fact they are perfectly secure from the pursuit of the wolf, bear, or even man himself." Meriwhether Lewis, Thursday, July 18, 1805

The Lewis and Clark expedition had many purposes. One of them was to record the fauna and flora of all the new land that Jefferson's Louisiana Purchase enveloped. "Record every new plant, animal, etc. that you come in contact with" were the orders Jefferson gave Lewis and Clark. The journals are filled with amazing new discoveries. Once, Lewis wrote, while observing a bighorn sheep on a steep cliff, that he marveled at how the design of that animal was so unique that it was safe in what appeared to be a dangerous and treacherous landscape. It was a fascinating observation.

> *"Even though I walk through the valley of the shadow of death, I fear no evil; for Thou art with me, Thy rod and Thy staff, they comfort me." Psalm 23:4*

It is interesting that an animal like the bighorn sheep can be at complete ease in such scary places. Its confidence lies within the unique design it was given.

We can learn a lot from those animals. There are times in life that seem as if we are about to fall off the edge of a cliff, and our whole world will come crashing down. These are times when the landscape of life shows no sign of easy terrain.

These are the times when we need to heed the words of King David. Just as those bighorn sheep can navigate the sides of cliffs due to their unique design, we can navigate with certainty through the cliffs of life because we are designed to rely upon a loving Father in heaven, who says, "I am with you. Do not worry. You are designed to depend on my faithfulness."

May we always rest in the faithfulness of God's promises to us, and may those promises of His ever-present presence be our comfort in our darkest times. As Lewis noted that the sheep were "perfectly secure" on a steep cliff, so are we perfectly secure at all times in God's loving care.

Questions for Reflection:

1. How has God designed you to be secure in Him?

2. Where do you find yourself trying to find security other than in Christ?

3. How can the truths found in this devotional be lived out in your life today?

RECOGNIZING HOME

"The Indian woman recognizes the country and assures us that this is the river on which her relations live." Meriwhether Lewis, July 22, 1805

During the cold winter with the Mandan Indians, Lewis and Clark hired an interpreter who brought his Shoshone wife named Sacajawea. This lady was one of the most important members of the expedition in many ways. One of them was that Lewis and Clark depended on her to lead them to her Shoshone people from whom she had been kidnapped years earlier by another tribe. The expedition needed horses to get through the treacherous rocky mountains, and they knew that the Shoshones were their only hope of acquiring them.

All rested on Sacajawea. As they got further into present day Montana, their spirits were lifted as Sacajawea began to recognize the terrain and landmarks. Lewis and Clark rested their hopes on Sacajawea's "recognition of home." As she began to recognize more and more, she knew she was getting closer to her home. The hopes of the expedition grew, until finally they met the long sought after Shoshone, who would then provide them with the horses they needed.

> *"He has made everything appropriate in its time. He has also set eternity in their heart, so that man will not find out the work which God has done from the beginning even to the end." Ecclesiastes 3:11*

From the moment they are born, every person since the beginning of time has been on a journey "home." God desires our home to be with him in eternity, and He has placed in man that beacon of "eternity" that helps us recognize the signs that show us the way to Him.

The sad thing is that man tries to hush that inner voice and blaze his own trails, while all along God is trying to show him the way. Recognize the terrain! Recognize the love of God, the grace of a loving Father, the compassion that says, "I accept you!"

85

Beware if you are searching for home in anything other than the love and redeeming message of Jesus Christ.

Home is our relationship with God, not a place on earth. Let the love of God, the inner voice He has placed in us and the map of the Scriptures guide us home.

Questions for Reflection:

1. What does it mean that man has "eternity within his heart"?

2. In what ways did God draw you to Him before you knew Him?

3. How can the truths found in this devotional be lived out in your life today?

MOSQUITOES, GNATS, AND PRICKLY PEARS

"Our trio of pests still invade and obstruct us on all occasions, these are the Musquetoes eye knats and prickley pears, equal to any three curses that ever poor Egypt laiboured under..." Meriwhether Lewis, July 24, 1805

The Corps of Discovery came up against many difficulties along the way to the Pacific: the bitter cold Dakota winters, the exhausting portage around the Great Falls of the Missouri, the extreme hunger experienced in the Bitteroot Mountains, the dismal wet winter of the Northwest. The list could go on and on, but possibly the greatest difficulties that wore on the men were the three listed above in Lewis's journal entry. They faced ever present daily annoyances that the outdoors inflicted upon them. The mosquitoes, the eye gnats, the prickly pears, these were with the men almost every day. They could not escape them, and over time these irritants wore on them so much that Lewis compared them to the plagues brought down on Egypt. Oh, the terrible reality of daily struggles!

> *"For the good that I wish, I do not do; but I practice the very evil that I do not wish."* Romans 7:19

Nothing is more difficult in following Jesus than the enemy's daily attacks on us through the weakness of our flesh. The flesh never gives up; it is there all the time, beckoning us to turn from Christ and give in to our sinful desires. It attacks our hearts, our minds, our eyes, and our motives.

So, how do we deal with the flesh? We don't. Christ, in the redeeming work of the cross and our daily sanctification, does! We are powerless on our own. We cannot "tough through it" like the Corps of Discovery toughed out the mosquitoes, gnats, and prickly pears.

Our strength in overcoming the daily attacks of the enemy actually rests in our inability to do just that. It is only Christ in our lives that can overcome the flesh. The redeeming quality in these daily struggles is that they make us realize we are helpless without

Christ, forcing us to put all our hope in Him. We need only to surrender and put on the things of Christ daily.

Questions for Reflection

1. In what ways do you find yourself trying to fight the flesh in your own strength?

2. How can you let your inability to conquer the flesh empower Christ's work in your life?

3. How can the truths found in this devotional be lived out in your life today?

PERFECT TIMING

"We begin to feel considerable anxiety with rispect to the Snake Indians. if we do not find them or some other nation who have horses I fear the successfull issue of our voyage will be very doubtfull or at allk events much more difficult in it's accomplishment." Meriwhether Lewis, July 27, 1805

The fate of the entire expedition rested on whether or not Lewis and Clark and their men could find the much sought after Shoshone Indians who they believed would provide them with the horses they would need to cross the rugged Rockies. From the time they met Sacajawea in Fort Mandan, they were resting their hopes on her helping them find her Shoshone people. This weighed heavily on their minds as the days passed, and they still had not found them. It was an issue of timing. The expedition needed those horses before the winter set in if they were to have a chance of getting through the Rockies. Thankfully, they ended up meeting the Shoshone in "perfect timing" that allowed them to use the horses they would need.

"My time is not yet here..." John 7:6

It is so easy to grow impatient, to look at the issues of life and try to rush the things of God because we think things need to be done in our timing, not God's. We try to force the Lord's timing in our lives to accommodate our impatience, all the while showing our utter ignorance of His perfect sovereign timing over every affair in our lives.

God has the timing of our lives in His perfect timing. He is in perfect control of our lives. Why do we find it so hard to trust His timing? He tells us not to be impatient, yet we are. He tells us there is a season for everything in our lives, yet we want to accept only the seasons when the sunshine of life shines the brightest, rather than when the dreary winters of life's unpredictable storms come at us.

We must trust that His timing for our lives is perfect. We need not worry or grow impatient with an unanswered prayer, because He promises to answer within His perfect timing.

Questions for Reflection:

1. In what ways are you not surrendering to God's timing in your life?

2. When you fully recognize that His timing is not yours, how does that affect your daily look at the circumstances you find yourself in?

3. How can the truths found in this devotional be lived out in your life today?

CONTENT PERSON

"Our Indian woman was one of the female prisoners taken at the time; tho' I cannot discover that she shews any immotion of sorrow in recollecting this event, or of joy being restored to her native country; if she has enough to eat and a few trinkets to wear I believe she would be perfectly content anywhere." Meriwhether Lewis, July 28, 1805

Of all the members of the expedition, none can surpass the greatness of the Shoshone woman Sacajawea. When Lewis and Clark reached the three forks of the Missouri River, they were in the location where years earlier Sacajawea had been kidnapped by Blackfeet Indians. At that time she witnessed the murders of beloved family members. We can imagine the images that played in her mind as they came upon the familiar ground. Despite the hell she had been through, her character seemed strong and resilient.

The entry above is a profound statement that reflects the character of Sacajawea. Even though she may not have expressed it, she was undoubtedly dealing with lots of emotions. To be fair, what person would not have strong emotions after having been through something like that? Yet, in spite of everything, Lewis recognized her as a person who seemed to be content with life.

> *"For we have brought nothing into this world so we cannot take anything out of it either. And if we have food and clothing with these we shall be content." 1 Timothy 6:7-8*

It is interesting to live in a world that has more stuff and things at the fingertips of man than ever before, yet man seems to be more empty and discontented with life than ever. Paul understood that contentment could never come in the form of material things. Although material things may bring temporal contentment, they cannot bring eternal contentment. He understood that contentment was something that could come only from within the deep rooted truth that we live in the knowledge of eternity.

91

Eternity with Christ is all that matters in the end. That is what we will have. All else will fall away, but our relationship with Jesus will last forever. Contentment must come from this simple truth. It can never be grasped in things, but it can be experienced in the person of Jesus Christ. He is our contentment, and whether we have much or little does not matter in the end.

Questions for Reflection:

1. How or in what ways are you putting your contentment into material things?

2. What ways can Jesus bring a contentment that the world cannot?

3. How can the truths found in this devotional be lived out in your life today?

PROPER CLOTHING

"All those who are not hunting altho'much fatiegued are busily engaged in dressing their skins, making mockersons lexing&c to make themselves comfortable." Meriwhether Lewis, July 28, 1805

The clothing the men of the expedition wore played a vital role. Life in the outdoors took a heavy toll on their clothing. They had to constantly make sure their clothing was adequate for whatever task was at hand and whatever weather came at them. They spent numerous hours sewing, patching and mending their clothes. Often, any free time they had would be occupied in those tasks. There were no stores to buy new things; the clothing they had was either made by them or received from native tribes.

Continual maintenance on their moccasins was key. Clothing could make or break their ability to keep going. Without the proper attire, the expedition would fail.

> *"And so, as those who have been chosen of God, holy and beloved, put on a heart of compassion, kindness, humility, gentleness and patience..."*
> *Colossians 3:12*

What clothes are we putting on each day? We are commanded to put on the things of God daily. The question is, "Do we?"

It would be utter foolishness to walk out in a blizzard in a tank top and pair of shorts; we would not be properly clothed. Do we not realize that putting the things of God on daily is so much more important! We were set free from the burden of sin and its snares. We not only received a new spirit, but we were given a new set of clothing! And God beckons us to put them on!

Why is it that we leave them in the closet, using them only when catastrophe hits? God says, "Put on compassion! Put on humility! Put on forgiveness!" These are the heavenly clothes that enable us to walk in freedom every day! Here is the key: we have the choice to put them on or not. It is up to us. God will never force us to get to the point of obedience. He desires our self-will to say yes to Him, for in that we show true love and respect. We need to

93

put on the heavenly clothes today, and tomorrow, and the next day. Choosing to put on the heavenly clothing is literally a matter of life or death.

Questions for Reflection:

1. How often do you willingly decide to clothe yourself as Colossians tells you to?

2. How does your decision to put on or take off these "clothes" affect your life?

3. How can the truths found in this devotional be lived out in your life today?

LOST AND FOUND

"Shannon had been dispatched up the rapid fork this morning to hunt, by Captclark before he met with Drewyeror learnt his mistake in the rivers. When he retunrned he sent Drewyer in surch of him, but he rejoined us this evening and reported that he had been several miles up the river and could find nothing of him. We had the trumpet sounded and fired several guns but he did not join this evening. i am fearful he is lost again." Meriwhether Lewis, August 6, 1805

Lewis wrote this in his journal in regard to Private George Shannon's second disappearance. Since so few men were on the expedition, it was evident that Lewis was very worried about whether Shannon would be found. In the wilds, who knew the odds? As leader of the expedition, Lewis had a heavy burden on his shoulders: one of his men was lost. He had to be found. Thankfully, a few days later, he *was* found, but those few days weighed heavily on Lewis's mind when one of his men was lost.

> *"But we had to be merry and rejoice, for this brother of yours was dead and has begun to live, and was lost and has been found." Luke 15:32*

Every day, the Lord looks at a lost world and weeps. He sees the lost people He created for His glory. He longs for them to be found in Him, and He beckons them to do so, but man chooses the selfish sin-stained way and remains lost.

Every day the heart of God must ache because His children are lost! But then, among the many who are lost, there are those who become found when they put their faith in Christ. The joy of the heart of God cannot be measured when one is found! He loves to see His children return home to Him.

Being found is a two-fold joy. First, it is a realization to the lost that they are no longer so, but are now in the safe arms of the Father. Second, it is the sincere joy the Father has when the original intent of man to be with Him is accomplished in one lost person being found.

Questions for Reflection:

1. Think about the day you gave your life to Jesus. Do you have the same joy for your salvation today as you did on that day?

2. How should knowing how it pleases the Father's heart when people turn to him inspire you to share the Gospel?

3. How can the truths found in this devotional be lived out in your life today?

ALL HOPES ARE GONE

"I now made a signal these men to halt, Drewyer obeyed but Shields who afterwards told me that he did not observe the signnal kept on..but he did not remain untill I got nearer than about 100 paces when he suddenly turned his horse about, gave him the whip leaped the creek and disapeared in the willow bruch in an instant and with him vanished all my hopes of obtaining horses for the preasent. I now felt quite as much mortification and disappointment as I had pleasure and expectation at the first sight of this indian." Meriwhether Lewis, August 11, 1805

The men had to find the Shoshone tribe. They needed horses to cross the Rockies. For months Lewis and his men worried about whether or not they could find the illusive tribe. If they did not get horses, the expedition was doomed. Finally, after what seemed an eternity, Lewis and two others on a scouting trip spotted what they believed to be a Shoshone Indian. The scene was tense...filled with anticipation. Approaching the Shoshone, one of the men, a man named Shields, did not see the signal Lewis gave indicating that they should halt. Because Shields kept moving forward, the much anticipated meeting of the Shoshone ended in disaster, as the Indian rode off on horseback into the woods.

> *"Be anxious for nothing, but in everything by prayer and supplication with thanksgiving let your requests be made known to God." Philippians 4:6*

So often we want to rush the plans of God in our lives. We do not see His guiding hand of wisdom telling us to wait. We do not hear His voice telling us to just stay and rest in Him. We do not see, hear or recognize Him telling us to halt! So we rush forward into our own plans, giving no adherence to His plans for us.

God's plans and timing for us are perfect, because He Himself is perfect. Why do we become anxious and move without His guidance? Probably because we think we know what is best for us, and our impatience is just another idol on our selfish altar of ego.

97

We must wonder how many missed opportunities we have had simply because we have shoved away God's plans by our impatience. We want to move forward, while God desires that we sit and wait. But the loving Father does not force us to wait; He allows us to make mistakes, so we can learn the lessons of His perfect plan.

Questions for Reflection:

1. In what ways do you generally tend to move forward in things rather than waiting on God?

2. How can understanding God's timing in your life help you in the way you plan and live life in general?

3. How can the truths found in this devotional be lived out in your life today?

DISAPPEARING TRACKS

"The track which we had pursued last evening soon disappeared."
Meriwhether Lewis, August 11, 1805

As the expedition traveled through the vast western frontier, there were times when they simply became lost. Despite the bountiful experience these woodsmen had, even they would lose their way. They had relied upon the Missouri River, old Indian trails and old maps that frontiersman had drawn up. But then, all of a sudden, the tracks and the trails they relied on would disappear, and they became lost, not knowing the way.

> *"Let Thy good Spirit lead me on level ground."* Psalm
> 143:10

As we walk with Jesus, there are those times when, for whatever reason, He remains silent. His still small voice that is a daily guide for us seems to vanish. We can't pick up the track of His leading, and all seems lost. What do we do during those quiet, seemingly endless times of His silence? What do we do during those times when His providential will for us remains obscure and hard to follow?

I suppose it would have been a walk in the park for Lewis and Clark to simply follow one track all the way to the Pacific. But then again, where would the *adventure* have been? What lessons would have been learned? Much the same, if the Christian walk were a simple well-staked out path, where would the lessons of trust in His plan come from? Where would the lessons of faith be? Where would we learn to rely on Him and not ourselves? Where would we learn to surrender to His divine plan, and, even more specific, where would we learn to surrender, to allow Him to reveal His plan to us in His timing?

The Lord's path for us is *His* path, not ours. He will always show us the way. He simply allows us the privilege of losing the "track" sometimes, so we can realize how helpless we are without Him.

99

Questions for Reflection:

1. How do you usually respond when God seems silent to your prayers?

2. How teachable are you in learning God's plans for your life when they don't match up with your own plans?

3. How can the truths found in this devotional be lived out in your life today?

ENCOURAGING WORDS

"The men in the water almost all day. they are weak soar and much fortiegued; they compained of the fortiegue to which the navigation subjected them and wished to go by land. Capt. C. encouraged them and passifyed them." Meriwhether Lewis, August 12, 1805

As the expedition moved on, there were times when the men grew tired and discouraged. Those times probably came often. It was during those times that Clark shined his brightest. There is a star quality in leadership that is often overlooked, and that is the ability to encourage. Lewis was known for being more temperamental than Clark, and I wonder if Lewis was growing weary of the men's complaining. I wonder how the expedition would have fared in situations like the one above if Lewis had dealt with it. Instead, we see Clark answer to the weary, tired and probably cranky men -- not with a rod of discipline, but with a compassionate encouraging word.

> *"Now may the God who gives perseverance and encouragement grant you to be the same mind with one another according to Christ Jesus." Romans 15:5*

The simplest things are often the most overlooked. Like an oasis in a dry desert, so is an encouraging word to a weary soul.

Romans says that God gives perseverance. We must conclude from this that there are going to be tough times through which we need to persevere. But God does not leave us. He doesn't let us persevere without providing encouragement. He knows that perseverance without encouragement is misery.

I imagine Jesus walking with his disciples and encouraging them through the hard times, encouraging them to "Go ahead and pray for that person and see what happens." He is the God of encouragement, and if He asks us to be of the same mind as He, then we have to place a priceless value on encouragement.

It is so simple, but so profoundly impactful, not only to be the receiver of encouragement, but also to be the giver, for in doing so, we are putting on the mind and attitude of Christ.

Questions for Reflection:

1. How often do you find yourself encouraging others?

2. What are some of the great encouragements that Jesus gives to you every day?

3. How can the truths found in this devotional be lived out in your life today?

FINDING THE SOURCE

"At the distance of 4 miles further the road took us to the most distant fountain of the waters of the Mighty Missouri in surch of which we have spent so many toilesome days and wristless nights. thus far I had accomplished one of those great objects on which my mind has been unalterably fixed for many years, judge then of the pleasure I felt in allayin my thirst with this pure and ice cold water..."Meriwhether Lewis, August 12, 1805

Finally, after thousands of miles, Lewis stood at the small fountain coming out of the earth that was the source of the Missouri River. As he drank from it, joy filled his heart. He had been searching for the source for a long time, and now, finally, all the hard work, all the pain and toil were brought into worthy fulfillment, as the joy of this accomplishment must have made all those things seem minute. Although disappointed by the reality that there was no all-water route from the Missouri to the Pacific, they had accomplished a great task by finding the source of the Missouri. The source had been found; that was all that mattered.

> *"For by Him all things were created, both in the heavens and on earth, visible and invisible, whether thrones or dominions or rulers or authorities--all things have been created by Him and for Him."* Colossians 1:16

The soul of sinful man is on a quest to find the source of life the moment he comes into the world. Like a deep inner longing, man knows within the depths of his being that the source of life cannot be found in anything that man can offer. His soul remains in a state of restlessness and misery until he finally has that great joyous day when he finds the true source of life, happiness, joy and contentment: Jesus Christ. He is the source of happiness, joy and contentment for all.

Life has many hard paths, many tough questions, many unseen obstacles, but they all lead to the Savior. Everything life throws at man cries out, "Return to the source!" Oh, that we would recognize the source of life every day! That we would not try to create a man-made source, but navigate the rivers of life to the love, forgiveness and grace found in Jesus Christ. When we find that source, there is no greater joy.

Questions for Reflection:

1. Think of your own testimony. In what ways did God call you to return to Him?

2. How impactful to you is the truth that Jesus connected you back to God?

3. How can the truths found in this devotional be lived out in your life today?

IT'S NOT MUCH

"The Chief informed us that they had nothing but berries to eat and gave us some cakes of serviceberries and Choke cherries which had been dryedin the sun." Meriwhether Lewis, August 13, 1805

When Lewis and Clark finally found the Shoshones, they realized quickly that food was scarce. The Shoshones did not have much food at all, but they shared what they did have. And from that act, a friendship was forged between the Shoshones and the expedition. Despite having so little at the time, the Shoshones gave some of the little they had to the Corps of Discovery. Selfless hospitality was shown.

> *"Philip answered Him, 'Two hundred denarii worth of bread is not sufficient for them, for everyone will receive a little.' One of His disciples, Andrew, Simon Peter's brother, said to Him, 'There is a lad here who has five barley loaves and two fish, but what are these for so many people?'" John 6:7-9*

One situation, two responses. When asked to feed the multitudes, Philip said, "No way. We simply do not have enough food." Then, when confronting the same challenge, Andrew saw a little boy with some food and said, "It's not much, but let's try this." Andrew took what little he had and committed it to God.

That is what separates people of faith from others. They see impossible tasks, take what little they have and cast it unto Jesus for His work, relying on His faithfulness, not their weakness. Oh, if we could have the perspective of Andrew and take those dreams God has placed in our hearts, look at our minimal abilities and say like Andrew, "It's not much, but let's try this!" Oh, what we would gain as we see God move mountains before our eyes!

The man of faith always rejoices in his limited ability, because it is another reminder of our helplessness without the Father's help. It may just be one lad with a few fish, but it is always a great God with an unlimited supply of His power.

Questions for Reflection:

1. When faced with problems, does your response show dependency on God?

2. How have you allowed your fears to limit what God wants to do in your life?

3. How can the truths found in this devotional be lived out in your life today?

LIFE'S NOT FAIR

"But that we did not ask either their horses or their services without giving a satisfactory compensation in return." Meriwhether Lewis, August 17, 1805

After finally finding the Shoshone Indians, Lewis and Clark were able to acquire the horses they would need to cross the Rockies. They wanted to make sure the Shoshones were compensated for the horses and their guides. In short, Lewis and Clark wanted to treat the Shoshones fairly in these dealings. They believed that if they were fair to the Indians, the favor would probably one day be returned. Being fair was important and held in high regard in this situation and the expedition, as they would need to continually make "business transactions" with the native tribes.

"There is therefore now no condemnation for those who are in Christ Jesus." Romans 8:1a

We have all heard the saying, "Life is not fair." Often we have personally felt the truth behind that statement at some point where we may have had the raw end of the deal or been wronged in an unfair way.

In fact, life is *not* fair. Some people are born into affluent countries that offer them amazing opportunities. Others are born into situations much gloomier and without much hope at all. Some people live long healthy lives; others suffer the tragic loss of a child to a terrible illness.

Life indeed is not fair. However, when we look at life's fairness through the eyes of Scripture, it is actually a good thing that life is not fair. The Bible says that all have sinned and fallen short of God's glory (Romans 3:23). We all deserve punishment, and yet we have a God who loves us so much He sent His one and only Son to take our punishment. He gave up all, to give us life. We deserved wrath; He gave us mercy. We deserve hell; He gives us heaven. If anything could be justified as not being fair, it would be Christ giving up His throne in heaven to die a terrible death.

May we tremble in awe and adoration that life is unfair in this regard. For if we were treated fairly when it comes to our sin, we would all be cut off from the presence of God forever.

Questions for Reflection:

1. In what areas has life seemed unfair to you?

2. What does Jesus do for you when life seems unfair?

3. How can the truths found in this devotional be lived out in your life today?

SOMBER REFLECTION

"This day I completed my thirty first year...I reflected that I had as yet done but little, very little indeed, to further the hapiness of the human race or to advance the information of the succeeding generation." Meriwhether Lewis, August 18, 1805

On his 31st birthday, Meriwhether Lewis wrote the above in his journal. This entry would become one of the most profound self-reflective entries he ever penned. Here is a guy, a former secretary to the President of the U.S., who was leading a historical expedition that would go down in history as one of the most epic expeditions ever, and yet he still reflected somberly upon his life. Lewis battled depression his whole life, and it led to his tragic death. Despite his struggle with depression, he was interested in passing on to future generations the lessons life had taught him, as well as the discoveries he had made. He wanted his life to bring change for the better. He most likely thought often of future generations and how his life could impact them for the better good.

> *"..not to look out for our own interests, but to look out for the interest of others." Philippians 2:4*

Since the fall in the garden, man has had the desire to serve himself. It is in the sin nature where the word "self" is prioritized, and the word "others" is not recognized. This is the way of the sin nature, always going against the ways of the Spirit.

Jesus poured out His life for others. He did not struggle with self to the degree we often do because it was others He desired to serve, most importantly His Father in heaven. He knew the greatest way to impact future generations was to lay down His life in service to mankind by pouring out His blood at Calvary. Through that death to self came life for others.

This is the way we are to live our lives. Daily we die to self, and through that "death," others are presented and blessed with the reflection of a Christ-focused life. Through that daily death to self, we are empowered to serve God, which then gives us life to serve others.

109

Questions for Reflection:

1. How often do you focus on "self" as opposed to "others"?

2. In what areas do you specifically need to die to self?

3. How can the truths found in this devotional be lived out in your life today?

WASTED TIME

"I viewed with regret the many hours I have spent in indolence, and now soarly feel the want of that information which those hours would have given me had they been judiciously expended."
Merriwhether Lewis, August 18, 1805

In this famous reflection on his 31st birthday, Lewis journaled about his own failings. It is hard to imagine a man so accomplished as Lewis viewing his life that way. I find it hard to imagine that he wasted *any* time, let alone to the extreme extent he noted. One thing we can say is that Lewis seemed to take his time on earth seriously.

> *"So teach us to number our days, that we may present to You a heart of wisdom." Psalm 90:12*

We have no idea how long we have on this earth. Today could very well be the last one we have. James likens our life to a vapor: Quick! Fleeting. Here and gone before we know it.

In our crazy, busy, instant gratification, fill-your-schedules-with-as-much-as-possible culture, I wonder how we have lost the appreciation of time, along with the wisdom of how to use that time. When we stand before Jesus, what will He say about how we spent our time on earth? Was it for Him? Was it spent furthering His kingdom? Was it utilized in a godly way?

David hit the nail on the head in Psalm 90. He realized that if we actually knew the day of our death, it most likely would bring a drastic change in our lives, and we would live more wisely.

What a reminder we have from this reflection of both Lewis and King David! Time is a gift. It is something we were entrusted and charged with; it is something of which we must be good stewards. Having hearts of wisdom starts with knowing that time is limited, so we must use it in a way that honors God.

111

Questions for Reflection:

1. How would you say you are spending the time God has given you on this earth?

2. In what ways can you better use your time here for His glory?

3. How can the truths found in this devotional be lived out in your life today?

SIT, SULK AND STAGNATE

"The guide informed us that a man might pass to the missouri from hence by that rout in four days." Meriwhether Lewis, September 9, 1805

After trudging through hard terrain to find the source of the Missouri, the expedition came to the Bitterroot Valley. It was here that their scout gave them the astonishing news that they *could* have arrived at that exact spot in four days, as opposed to the 52 it took them. Instead of four days, it took them 53!

Imagine the realization of all the hard work, long days and hungry times that could have been avoided had they known that route. Imagine the "if we only" scenarios that played in their minds. At a time in the expedition when men were at utter exhaustion, the news probably hit them like a ton of bricks.

It was at this point that they had four choices: they could sit and ponder what opportunity they missed; they could begin to cast blame on each other; they could continually go back to the past and say, "If only we had done this, or if only we had been more observant"; or they could press forward and move on, realizing that what was in the past was in the past.

> *"How much more will the blood of Christ, who through the eternal Spirit offered Himself without blemish to God, cleanse your conscience from dead works to serve the living God." Hebrews 9:14*

Satan uses no strategy more than bringing up our past failings to hinder our walk with Christ. Time and time again, he throws our failures and shortcomings at us, hoping to get us to sit, sulk, and stagnate.

That's what happens when we hold onto the past wrongs we have committed. We sit, allowing our faith to be immobile and ineffective. We sulk, feeling sorry for ourselves. We stagnate and begin to lose our passion for Christ; we stop sharing Him with others.

113

We must cling to the above truth that our shortcomings were dealt with on Calvary, and our consciences from these dead works should be clear so we may serve Jesus all the more! We must embrace the power of the cross and walk in the truth that our consciences have been freed to serve the living God!

Questions for Reflection:

1. How many times do you remind yourself of your failures? How does that hinder your walk with Jesus?

2. What has Jesus' death on the cross done for your conscience?

3. How can the truths found in this devotional be lived out in your life today?

COMMON LANGUAGE

"Our guide could not speake the language of these people but soon engaged them in conversation by signs and jesticulation, the common language of all the Aborigines of North America." *Meriwhether Lewis, September 10, 1805*

Communication was one of the difficult things Lewis and Clark battled about with the native tribes. Although they had interpreters, those interpreters often did not speak the language of the tribe they were in contact with. Thus, they had to rely on sign language, which apparently was understood by most tribes all across the continent. If it were not for this "common language" of hand signs, history might have taken a different route many times during the expedition. Through this "common language," Lewis and Clark were able to properly communicate their motives and demands to each tribe they encountered, and vice versa.

"This is my command, that you love one another, just as I have loved you." John 15:12

The only way to connect a Holy God to a sinful man is through love. Man is so far from the righteousness of God that the connection has to come from a perfect love. The way a redeemed person connects with one stuck in sin is through love. Love is the way God connected us back to Him, and it is the way He desires us to connect with others.

Love is not an option; it is a command from our Lord and Savior. We do not have the right to *not* love someone. If we believe we do, then we claim we are more lovable to a Holy God than others. This wreaks of self-righteousness and hypocrisy. We do not have the option not to love, because Jesus went to the cross even for those who appear unlovable.

He commands us to love others as He has loved us. How does He love us? In our wretched sin. In our rank ugliness. In our small, selfish, ungodly world, He loves us. He loves us sacrificially. He puts our interests before His own.

115

Love is the common language of the souls of man, for every soul on earth longs to be connected through love. Everyone longs to be connected to the One who gives ultimate love. Every soul longs for this great gift.

Questions for Reflection

1. In what way does God communicate His love to you the most?

2. In what ways can you fall into self-righteousness and hypocrisy?

3. How can the truths found in this devotional be lived out in your life today?

LOOK TO THE HORIZON

"From this mountain I could observe high rugged mountains in every direction as fas as I could see." William Clark, September 16, 1805

This entry was written during the hard trek through the Bitterroot Mountains. It was a point of desperation in the expedition. The men were cold, hungry, sick and exhausted. They were desperate to find the valleys where they had hoped to find the Nez Perce Indians. Imagine the discouragement that Clark must have felt as he climbed to the top of that high mountain, hoping to see the end of those rugged devils, only to see more of them as far as the eye could see. We can almost hear him sigh, take a deep breath, bow his head, and stare at the ground, wondering when they would ever get through. Doubt crept in. "My goodness, when will we ever get through these mountains?" he must have thought a thousand times.

> *"Do you not know that those who run in a race all run, but only one receives the prize? Run in such a way that you may win." 1 Corinthians 9:24*

When we walk with Jesus, there are times when He allows us to be on that mountaintop. He gives us the privilege of having those divine times in life where nothing could be better. We sit on that mountaintop and bask in His glory. We desire to stay there.

But "No," says our Savior. He says, "Look out to the horizon." We look, and before us we see mountains upon mountains of hard life. We see all the things that will swallow us whole.

He tells us again, "Look to the horizon!" We again look at the mountains. "To the horizon!" He shouts. Finally, we look to the horizon, and we see Him! All of a sudden, the mountains are mere bumps along the path of life.

We must learn to fix our eyes on Jesus. We must learn to not focus on the mountains of life, but on the Giver of life. He has placed the mountains to get us to focus on the horizon. When we focus on the mountains, they remain mountains. When we focus on

117

the horizon where Jesus is, then we win. We win every time. The mountains are not so big anymore, but rather a way to draw us closer to the Savior.

Questions for Reflection:

1. What mountains have you been focusing on in your life that may be distracting you from Jesus?

2. Why would God place mountains, valleys, and deserts in our lives?

3. How can the truths found in this devotional be lived out in your life today?

LOW POINT

"I have been wet and as cold in every part as I ever was in my life, indeed I was at one time fearfull my feet would freeze in the thin Mockirsons which I wore..." William Clark, September 16, 1805

Clark was at a low point. The expedition was taking a huge toll on his body physically and emotionally. It was during these hard times where their characters were not only tested, but also refined for future trials.

> *"Who is this that hides counsel without knowledge? Therefore I have declared that which I did not understand, Things too wonderful for me, which I did not know." Job 42:3*

What man can understand the ways of an Almighty God? How foolish to ponder the thought that we mortal men can comprehend the master plan of our sanctification. For if we were able to understand His ways of making us more like Him, our understanding would for sure exclude suffering and hardship. Why would we even consider putting those two things into the equation, for they make no sense to us in our limited comprehension?

But God is able to use what He wants to use to mold us into His likeness, and it is often through hardship and suffering that this takes place. Why? We have no idea. We can only trust in His divine wisdom that the trials we go through are meant for a greater purpose than we can comprehend.

The man who is able to say, "God, have your way in me...in whatever way that may be" is a saint who has entrusted all to God and abandoned the thought of knowing what is best for him. It is God who may do as He pleases, but, in doing what He pleases as He draws us nearer to Him, He does not leave us helpless, but supplies the grace to endure and abound through those trials. Trials and hardships bring forth the glory of God into the lives of those who can understand this hard truth.

Questions for Reflection:

1. Think about a low point in your life. How did God help you through that time and what did you learn from it?

2. How does entrusting our entire lives to His will and purposes free us?

3. How can the truths found in this devotional be lived out in your life today?

ONE OLD WOMAN

The explanation below is of an event that was never recorded in the journals of Lewis and Clark because they had no idea the event ever occurred. It was passed down from the oral tradition of the Nez Perce. The story is amazing and worthy to be noted. September 1805

Probably one of the lowest points for the expedition was when Lewis and Clark finally made it through the Bitterroot Mountains. In 11 exhausting days, they travelled 165 miles in unforgivable terrain.

When they finally made it out of the mountains, they were met by the Nez Perce tribe. Since these were most likely the first white people the Nez Perce had seen, they held a council under the leadership of Twisted Hair. There was talk of killing Lewis and Clark and all the members of the expedition and taking all their goods.

An old lady in the village named Watkuweis warned them not to kill the whites, and she shared her story of how she had been kidnapped long ago by the Blackfeet, and then sold to a white trader, who apparently treated her well and better than the Blackfeet. She then escaped from the white trader and returned to her people. She told Twisted Hair and the other Nez Perce not to harm the whites, for the whites had treated her well. That one act of intercession saved the lives of Lewis and Clark.

> *"Yet He has now reconciled you in His fleshly body through death, in order to present you before Him holy and blameless and beyond reproach." Colossians 1:22*

Never underestimate how one act of intercession affects history. It changed history for Lewis and Clark.

It changed the eternity of the souls of man through Jesus Christ interceding on our behalf.

What a reminder of the sentence of death we all had on us and that, through one amazing act of intercession, that sentence was cancelled. Jesus *was* and *is* the ultimate intercessor. We deserved death; He stepped in out of the shadows of perfection and gave us life. We can never stop exploring the depth and truth behind that act of sacrifice.

But it does not stop with Jesus interceding on our behalf. We also get the privilege of walking in our faith daily and interceding for others through our prayers, our actions and our callings.

Questions for Reflection:

1. How did the one act of Jesus dying on the cross affect humanity?

2. Knowing the significance of our actions, how should we live our lives as lights to the world?

3. How can the truths found in this devotional be lived out in your life today?

ROOM CHANGER

"The sight of This Indian woman, wife to one of our interprs. confirmed those people of our friendly intentions, as no women ever accompanies a war party of Indians in this quarter." William Clark, October 19, 1805

Sacagawea literally saved the expedition on more than a few occasions. This lady, through her knowledge of the land, her gift of languages, and simply the fact that she was a woman, proved to be a huge advantage to the Corps of Discovery.

At times during the expedition Lewis and Clark were not sure how native tribes would receive them. Would it be peacefully or with hostility? As they approached new tribes, simply having Sacagawea with them as the only female member of the expedition was a clear sign to the tribes that they meant no harm and were not a war party. Her presence changed the atmosphere for the better in their situations.

> *"And when they did not find them, they began dragging Jason and some brethren before the city authorities shouting, 'These men who have upset the world have come here also.'" Acts 17:6*

Jesus changed the atmosphere when He was present. He would take the darkest place and turn it into a bright one. Being the Son of God, He carried the light with Him, and He did not have to do anything to change the area around Him; it simply changed because His character demanded it.

The disciples were known for being those who "upset the world" because, wherever they went, they boldly carried His name. As we walk in this life, we have the living God inside of us, and we carry with us the Person who changes the atmosphere of the room, the town, the city, or the nation we are in, simply because He abides within us.

Are we room changers? Does the spiritual atmosphere of the place we are in change as we carry His presence? Or are we so full of self that His image within us is so blurred and foggy that it cannot shine forth as intended?

Questions for Reflection:

1. How do our daily decisions affect the capacity to which we become room changers?

2. How boldly do you proclaim the name of Jesus in your life?

3. How can the truths found in this devotional be lived out in your life today?

GOING WITH THE CURRENT

"We made 42 miles to day; the current much more uniform than yesterday or the day before." William Clark, October 20, 1805

It is amazing how much ground the expedition covered when weather was good and the currents of the rivers were in their favor. Half of their journey was spent going up river, against the current. We can imagine the joy when the currents began to take their boats in the proper direction, allowing the men to rest their weary arms. The day's toil was eased, as the currents did most of the work.

> *"But I say, walk by the Spirit, and you will not carry out the desire of the flesh." Galatians 5:16*

Man is designed to be led by the Holy Spirit. The original intent for Adam in the garden was perfect leading by God. Adam's life had a natural flow where everything he did was a true act of worship, rooted in his being led by the Spirit.

When we allow the leading of the Spirit in our lives, we are united with our original purpose: to be led by God in everything. Although stained with sin, when we make that conscious decision to allow the Holy Spirit to lead us, we empower God's work in our lives. We hear Him more clearly, we obey Him without hesitation; we shudder at the mere thought of sin in thought, word, or deed. We are flowing in what we were naturally designed for: complete obedience to the Father.

He knows where we need to be, how we need to get there, and how much time it will take. Why do we not take hold of His promise and let Him take us through the rivers of life? We must *choose* to do this; we must take every step to continue to walk in the Spirit. Christ puts us there on Calvary, but we have to navigate the dusty, dirty road of life, making that daily choice to walk in the Spirit.

Questions for Reflection:

1. Looking at your life, how much of it is led by the Spirit?

2. Jesus tells us if we are led by the Spirit, it will have a profound impact on our lives. Do you see that impact on your life?

3. How can the truths found in this devotional be lived out in your life today?

OH, THE JOY!

"Ocean in view! Oh, the joy! This great Pacific Ocean which we been so long anxious to See." William Clark, 1805

One can only imagine the pure joy William Clark had when he wrote this entry in his journal. After trudging across the continent, through toils and dangers that stagger the imagination, they finally had reached the ocean. Although this entry was describing a bay and not the actual ocean, the spirit of Clark's writings expresses a joy that only one who has come through difficult times could express. They had made it! The joy must have been overwhelming. We can imagine the tears welling up in Clark's eyes. It was a monumental time!

> *"Restore to me the joy of Thy salvation, And sustain*
> *me with a willing spirit." Psalm 51:12*

There is no greater tragedy in the Christian walk than the loss of the joy of our salvation. This tragedy does not occur at a specific time, but it comes slowly, over the daily battles we fight as we follow Jesus.

Over time, we lose the realization of two main things: who we once were and what we were rescued from. If we keep these two realities in front of us daily, then we can do nothing but experience the joy of His salvation every waking moment.

The joy of our salvation can be realized only when we recognize what we have been saved from and whom we have been saved from: hell and ourselves. The joy of our salvation is the greatest joy man can know. It is the pinnacle of all roads to contentment and must always be. David realized this when he asked the Lord to give him a willing spirit to recognize this truth and walk in this joy. Oh, the joy of our salvation!

Questions for Reflection:

1. How often do you ask the Lord to restore to you the joy of your salvation?

2. How does remembering who we once were and who we are now empower the work of the Holy Spirit within us?

3. How can the truths found in this devotional be lived out in your life today?

MASTERS

"Those Indians are certainly the best Canoe navigators I ever saw. rained all day." William Clark, November 11, 1805

Clark's entry shows the respect he had for the coastal tribe he alluded to. As they approached the Pacific, they were amazed at the ease with which the natives maneuvered their canoes. Navigating in the handmade log cut-out canoes was not an easy task, and the men of the expedition battled it the entire time. But the natives had it down, and it was definitely a result of their being better equipped for that style of travel. Over the years, through practice and necessity, they had become equipped to be masters of the canoe.

> *"Preach the word, be ready in season and out of season, reprove, rebuke, exhort, with great patience and instruction." 2 Timothy 4:2*

The charge we are given here is to be ready and equipped with the Gospel. We are to be masters of knowing how to implement the message of the Gospel at all times and in all places.

To be equipped means to stand ready. To be equipped means to be confident. To be equipped means to know the times. Are we masters of the message of the Gospel? Do we walk in this life confident and prepared with the greatest news on earth?

Many of us have become numb to the discipline of knowing the Gospel so we can share it with others. We sadly know the Gospel so we can save it for ourselves. This is the tragedy, and this is why Timothy is charged to get equipped to share! Get equipped, and be ready in all seasons with the Gospel. Become a master of the Gospel. How much our world would change if all of us who were masters of our trades would put as much focus into becoming masters of the Gospel.

Questions for Reflection:

1. Would you consider yourself prepared to share and defend the Christian faith?

2. Is the Gospel in your life being shared with others?

3. How can the truths found in this devotional be lived out in your life today?

STOPS IN THE RAIN

"Some intervals of fair weather last night, rain continued this morning." William Clark, November 13, 1805

As the men wintered at Fort Clatsop in the Pacific Northwest, they were brought to the end of their rope by the dismal conditions. Rain would simply not stop; it rained all the time. It is easy to imagine how that could take a toll on people who were constantly living in the outdoors. But even with the continual rain, every now and then a glimmer of hope would come, as the sun would shine and allow a few hours for the men to get out of the fort, hunt, and dry their clothes and goods. These small stops in the rain and beams of sunshine provided the extra push the men needed to continue through to the next day, during that long winter before their return to the East.

> *"And He said to me, 'My grace is sufficient for you, for power is perfected in weakness.'" 2 Corinthians 12:9*

What we need to see here is that this is personal. Paul said, "He said to me..." Jesus was addressing the individual Paul, in his individual situation of being stretched via a thorn in his flesh that brought him to his wit's end. Jesus always does this...He *addresses* us. He does not look at the crowd around us; He looks at the person within us and tells us He has brought us where we are to learn dependence on Him. No matter what situation we find ourselves in, He promises sufficient grace, not only to make it through, but to experience His power through it. True power comes through knowing our own weakness and *His* strength.

We cannot find His strength by focusing on *our* strength. It is by being brought to the end of our ropes that we find the beginning of His true power in allowing us the privilege of experiencing *His* grace. No matter how hard the times, Jesus gives us that break in the weather to experience His grace that will empower us to get through the storm triumphantly.

131

Questions of Reflection:

1. How does knowing the sufficiency of God's grace affect your life?

2. In what ways do you tend to lean on your own strength rather than God's?

3. How can the truths found in this devotional be lived out in your life today?

CARVING ON A TREE

"Here I found Capt. Lewis name on a tree. I also engraved my name, and by land the day of the month and year, as also Several of the men." William Clark, November 18, 1805

They had made it to the Pacific. All the blood, sweat, and tears had paid off, as they looked out and saw the crashing waters of the Pacific punish the rocky coastline. In classic fashion, like little kids with pocketknives, the men etched their names into a tree to leave a mark of this great feat on the pages of history. Imagine the tears welling up in their eyes as they carved each letter. A monumental time in all their lives was being carved into a lonely tree on a coastline. They had to leave a mark, a legacy, a symbol of remembrance.

> *"According to my earnest expectation and hope, that I shall not be put to shame in anything, but that with all boldness, Christ shall even now, as always, be exalted in my body, whether by life or by death." Philippians 1:20*

It is engrained into the soul of man to leave a legacy. All of us desire to be remembered for something. We want to make sure that when we leave this temporal earth, something "of us" continues on.

For the Christian, this mark to be left behind must be the story of the resurrected Savior in the life of a sinner. It is a powerful and worthy legacy any of those who follow Christ can leave behind. It is powerful and worthy because, when the world looks at our corpses in the ground, they will not see dead bodies, but fully alive stories of how Jesus Christ was glorified in us.

Ah, to leave this world with a legacy that shouts, "I once was lost, but now am found!" It is a legacy that never ends and passes on to generation after generation. What legacy are we building on this earth? When others look at our legacy, will they see only memories of us, or will they see a legacy that directs them to see the Savior in all His glory?

Questions for Reflection:

1. How can you begin to leave a "Christ Legacy" on this earth?

2. When people look at your life after you are long gone, what is it you desire them to remember most of all?

3. How can the truths found in this devotional be lived out in your life today?

WORTHY OF NOTICE

"Nothing worthy of notice occured today." Meriwhether Lewis, January 29, 1806

As the men endured the hard rainy winter at Fort Clatsop, the days became monotonous. In this journal entry Lewis shows the state of affairs. It was a difficult time, a time when the only thing they noticed was how much it was raining and how little they could accomplish. It took effort to notice things worthy to record in their journals during this time.

> *"Sing to the Lord a new song; Sing to the Lord, all the earth. Sing to the Lord, bless his name; Proclaim good tidings of His salvation from day to day." Psalm 96:1-2*

There is never a moment of the day, never a time in our lives or a period we are going through that should not say, "Praise be to you, oh Lord!" When we know Jesus, everything we are privileged to experience is worthy of the highest praise and worthy of our notice. Whether a cup of coffee, a cool crisp morning, or a pillow to lay our heads on, we have reason to praise Him.

God gave Adam and Eve complete contentment in the garden; they lacked nothing. All around them declared the glory of God, and yet they strayed. They became disillusioned into thinking the creation of God was not enough for their praises.

No, they desired selfishness, and it stained the focus of the praise of man forever. We have an amazing opportunity to recognize the Savior in all things, for all things come from Him. Let us not stop recognizing and marveling at His majesty and beauty in all things, from the simplest smile of a child with an ice cream cone to the grandest mountain on the earth. These things are worthy of our praise to Him.

Questions for Reflection:

1. How can you develop "patterns of praise" in your life?

2. Why is it important to praise the Lord even during the hard times?

3. How can the truths found in this devotional be lived out in your life today?

SMALLPOX

"I think the late ravages of the small pox may well account for the number of remains of vilages which we find deserted on the river and Sea coast in this quarter." Meriwhether Lewis, February 7, 1806.

Coming upon empty villages that once were inhabited by native tribes must have been an eerie sight. Smallpox took a terrible toll on the native tribes; entire villages were destroyed because of this terrible disease that the European white man had brought. Smallpox was only one of the many diseases that plagued the natives, as well as the white man. And the more the two interacted, simply through the transference of a cold or the blatant immoral relations between the two, disease spread. One person's act of ignorance and selfishness could have drastic effects on the multitudes.

> *"Through one transgression there resulted condemnation to all men..." Romans 5:18*

Followers of Jesus can never take sin lightly. They can never brush it off lightly. Sin in our lives is never a personal thing. It is always corporate in that our sin affects others around us in ways we never know.

Adam and Eve could not have known their one act of sin would result in eternal condemnation of the multitudes. Through that one act, the consequences have reigned down from generation to generation. It is easy to look at Adam and Eve and mock them for their behavior; it is easy to distance ourselves from them, but what if that "simple sin" we committed today has consequences that echo for generations to come?

We must not take sin lightly. Its consequences are selfish; its ending is hurt, and its aftereffects are ruined relationships, inner toil and destroyed lives.

Questions for Reflection:

1. Do you ever find yourself taking sin in your life lightly? What is the danger in that attitude?

2. How can you become more aware of what sins you are taking lightly in your life?

3. How can the truths found in this devotional be lived out in your life today?

ONE CANOE

"We yet want another canoe, and as the Clatsops will not sell us one at a price which we can afford to give we will take one from them in lue of the six Elk they stole from us in the winter." Meriwhether Lewis, March 1806

Lewis and Clark led the expedition with the highest standards and integrity. For the most part they dealt with the natives as fairly as they could, and neither of them took part in the promiscuous life that many of the other men did with the native women. Then, a chink in their armor of upstanding character was found when they decided to steal a canoe from the Clatsop Indians. They justified it by saying it was in response to the thievery the Clatsops had performed on them earlier. No matter how one looks at it, they stole. And through this one act, an almost flawless character of leadership was compromised.

> *"Therefore, as one trespass led to condemnation for all men, so one act of righteousness leads to justification and life for all men." Romans 5:18*

We can never underestimate the power behind on act of disobedience to God. We cannot grasp the consequences of our actions when they are not of Him. When we look in the garden, we see that the fruit was so much more than fruit. Until that point, Adam and Eve had an unblemished record, but they let their guard down, and we all have suffered the consequences.

We must remind ourselves that we are one bad decision away from tarnishing the work of God within us. It is not something to be taken lightly. When we give in to sin, the consequence is always more and deeper than we imagined, even if we do not see it at the time.

The power of one act is amazing. One act led to the death of man. One act led to the redemption of man. Never underestimate the power and consequence of one act.

Questions for Reflection:

1. Have you ever considered that your sins, though maybe small in your eyes, have terrible consequences, even though you may not see them at the time?

2. When it comes to decision-making in your life, do you find yourself ever thinking of the good or bad consequences those decisions may have?

3. How can the truths found in this devotional be lived out in your life today?

ABIDE OR DIVIDE

"Our party also too small to think of leaving any of them to return to the U'States by sea, particularly as we shall be necessarily divided into three or four parties on our return in order to accomplish the objects we have in view." Meriwhether Lewis, March 18, 1806

As the expedition readied itself to make the return trip to the East, they had to make the critical decision to stay as one unit, rather than sending some members back by sea across the ocean. They knew they would have to divide their men eventually, so to divide them even further at the beginning of the return trip would have been a careless idea. At this time they realized that they needed to abide with each other, as a larger group. Dividing the group was not an option, as it would have made them more vulnerable to many dangers. Later, when Lewis and Clark did break up into two parties, it almost cost some of them their lives, and it did end up costing the lives of two Blackfeet Indians.

"I am the vine, you are the branches; he who abides in Me, and I in him, he bears much fruit; for apart from Me you can do nothing." John 15:5

We were created to be together and dependent on Jesus. He is our vine, our source of life. We are the branches, completely dependent on him, utterly helpless without Him. To dare and imagine a life without Christ on our own, separated, is to ponder and dance with death.

We were created not only to abide in Him, but, as a result of that, to bear much fruit. Not *some* fruit, but *much* fruit. This can come only when we choose to abide in Him, rather than go off on our own. When we take that path, it always leads to death because, if we as branches are dependent on the vine, how can we continue to live without our source of spiritual nourishment? It is impossible.

This is why Jesus took 11 verses in John 15 to illustrate this truth. Those who abide thrive; those who divide die. We can choose to divide ourselves from the vine, but in the end we are greeted by

141

spiritual death. We must abide in Him, for in doing so we find life, nourishment and a fruitful ministry. We must also realize that our fruit bearing is based on the truth that He indeed abides in us. Any fruit we see is His work in our lives. It is always His work in our lives that bears fruit in our lives.

Questions of Reflection:

1. What does it mean to "abide in Christ"?

2. How do abiding in Christ and bearing fruit in your life and ministry relate to each other?

3. How can the truths found in this devotional be lived out in your life today?

THE LONG HAUL

"The object of this list is, that through the medium of some civilized person who may see the same, it may be known to the informed world, that the party consisting of the persons whose names are hereunto annexed, and who were sent out by the government of the U'States in May 1804. to explore the interior of the Continent of North America, did penetrate the same by way of the Missouri and Colombia Rivers, to the discharge of the latter into the Pacific Ocean, where they arrived on the 14th of November 1805, and from whence they departed the day of March 1806 on their return to the United states by the same rout they had come out." Meriwhether Lewis, March 18, 1806

Lewis and Clark were men who finished what they started. When they left the East in 1804, they were in it for the long haul. Failure was not an option. They knew many hardships lay in their future, but they were not deterred. They were men with an amazing resolve to finish.

> *"I have fought the good fight, I have finished the course, I have kept the faith." 2 Timothy 4:7*

The Christian life is one that demands people who are in it for the long haul. There is nothing half-hearted about Jesus' command to leave all to follow Him. We must always look at our daily walk with Jesus as a small part of an eternal walk with Him.

We desire immediate sanctification in our hearts and immediate change in our minds, but that is not what God does with us. Like a rough rock in a stream that is slowly shaped by the continual flow of water, so our spirits are slowly shaped over time by the Holy Spirit. To become like Jesus takes time, plain and simple. It takes success and failure. It demands perseverance and struggle.

For in those things our characters are forged to depend on Jesus for everything. When we understand that God's timing is perfect in our lives, and He is working on us for His purposes, then we are able to stay with confidence in the walk of faith in Him.

143

Questions for Reflection:

1. Why is the Christian life one that requires those with perseverance?

2. Does your walk resemble a marathon or a sprint?

3. How can the truths found in this devotional be lived out in your life today?

GETTING UNDERWAY

"I expect when we get under way we shall be much more healthy. it has always had that effect on us heretofore." Meriwhether Lewis, March 20, 1806

All they wanted was to get going and start their trek back east. But the terrible weather, lack of food, and poor health of the men prevented the Corps of Discovery from beginning their trip back. The inability to get going and get "underway" had a direct impact on the men's health and motivation. The longer they sat and did nothing, the worse they became. The more they kept moving and stayed busy, the healthier they were, mentally and physically. Daily life without challenge or change dulled the men in spirit and body.

> *"And do not be conformed to this world, but be transformed by the renewing of your mind, that you may prove what the will of God is, that which is good and acceptable and perfect." Romans 12:2*

The life of a follower of Jesus must be continually moving and growing. We were not created to stay the same. We were created by the power of the Holy Spirit to change.

A key factor in our becoming like Christ is not letting our minds grow dull and stagnate. Our minds must be all about the things of God. Our minds must be renewed daily by allowing the Holy Spirit to control us and reign in our spirits.

We seek direction, but find none. We ask God to show us His will, but we hear nothing. We strive to want to live a life for Christ, but end up disappointed.

We must ask ourselves, "Are our minds being renewed daily by the things of God? Are our minds being cleared of the stuff that keeps us from hearing from God?" Our minds were created to change daily, to be continually exercised in the things of God. When we keep our minds active in the things of God, then the result will be our clearer understanding of His perfect will.

145

Questions for Reflection:

1. Does your daily life allow time for the renewing of your mind in the things of God?

2. What ways can you intentionally focus on renewing your mind?

3. How can the truths found in this devotional be lived out in your life today?

DAILY SUSTENANCE

"This information gave us much uneasiness with rispect to our future means of susbsistence. Above the falls or through the plains from thence to the Chopunnish there are no deer Antelope nor elk on which we can depend for subsistence." Meriwhether Lewis, April 1, 1806

As the expedition began their return east, they spent some time on present day Sauvie's Island on the Columbia River to hunt and gather as much food as possible, since they were worried that little food lay ahead. Obviously, Lewis was very concerned about the lack of food for the future, and it was no wonder, considering the near starvation they had experienced on their way west. They needed food to give them energy to get back. Daily sustenance was a huge concern during the entire expedition.

> *"It is written, 'Man shall not live on bread alone, but on every word that proceeds out of the mouth of God.'" Matthew 4:4*

The spirit of man was created to be nourished solely by God. Likewise, the spirit of man cut off from the life found in Christ is destined for death. This is where we fail, by believing the lie of Satan who whispers in our ears that our spirits can find nourishment elsewhere.

Jesus, after 40 days with no water or food, demonstrated the truth that our spirits can survive only through God. Allowing God's word to nourish us brings life to our spirits, just as a river brings life to a dry plain. This is what our spirits were designed for, so why do we look elsewhere for that nourishment? Is it because we do not believe God's word? Is it because we put ourselves in God's seat and think we know what is best for us? Or is it utter rebellion? I dare to think that at times it may be all three. This is why our spirits remain sick: we look for nourishment everywhere except the Word of God, which is where we were designed to find it.

<u>Questions for Reflection:</u>

1. How often do you choose the Word of God as your daily spiritual nourishment?

2. If you were to do a "spiritual physical," would you be healthy or in need of surgery?

3. How can the truths found in this devotional be lived out in your life today?

NEW VISION

"I observed the Indian woman who visited us yesterday blind of an eye, and a man who was nearly blind of both eyes. the loss of sight I have observed to be more common among all the nations inhabiting this river than among any people I ever observed."
William Clark, April 8, 1806

Among the vast amounts of information the Corps of Discovery was recording were the observations they made of the many native tribes they came in contact with. In this particular tribe, Clark noticed a common issue of bad eyesight, which he later ascribed to the fact that the tribe lived right on the Columbia River, and the glare off the water was so strong. For whatever reason, these people seemed to have poor vision. Whether a result of the climate, sun, or diet, their vision was inhibited in ways that caused Clark to make an entry in his journal.

> *"Then Elisha prayed and said, 'O Lord I pray, open his eyes that he may see.' And the Lord opened the servant's eyes, and he saw; and behold, the mountain was full of horses and chariots of fire all around Elisha."* 2 Kings 6:17

The redeemed man is a man who has a new vision. He sees things through the eyes of Christ, no longer through the eyes of selfishness and sin. When we abide in Christ and ask Him to give us new spiritual vision, then we begin to see things representing Him all around us. We no longer need to ask the Lord to show us whom to serve, for we are seeing the needs of others through this new vision.

To have our vision realigned, we must do two things: receive and focus. We need to receive in faith the new spiritual vision Christ has given us as truth and reality of the new redeemed self. Then we must daily focus our eyes on Him and toward the heavenly things. The more we focus there, the easier our sight on earth will be. We will see the things of God all around us, and through this we will be

149

encouraged, challenged and spurred on to good deeds. Oh, that we would realize the new vision we have!

<u>Questions for Reflection:</u>

1. How is your "spiritual eyesight"? Are you viewing life through the new vision Christ has given you?

2. How should focusing on Jesus daily affect the way you view the world?

3. How can the truths found in this devotional be lived out in your life today?

GOOD NEWS IS COMING

"There was great joy with the nativs last night in consequence of the arrival of the salmon; one of the fish was cought, this was the harbenger of good news to them." -William Clark, April 19, 1806

The tribes of the Columbia River were dependent upon the salmon as one of their primary food sources. If the salmon did not run, they did not survive. So it is no wonder that excitement came over the camp each year with the promised return of the salmon. The arrival of the salmon literally brought good news and joy to everyone. One cannot imagine how devastating it would have been to the coastal river tribes had the salmon not returned.

> *"For I am not ashamed of the gospel, for it is the power of God for salvation to everyone who believes, to the Jew first and also to the Greek."*
> *Romans 1:16*

We are called to be room changers and atmosphere makers. That is one of the job descriptions for those who follow Christ. When we enter rooms, do those around us see the good news that just walked in? When we live in a town or city, do we bring good news to the area?

As followers of Jesus, we are under the world's magnifying glass, and the world will do anything it can to find fault in our convictions to follow Him. May we never be accused of bringing anything other than good news to lost men! The good news the Christian brings is literally the difference between life and death to all who hear, because the good news is His story.

Do we bring good news to others? Do the lost and hurting around us anticipate our return, knowing that when we return, so will the good news? We cannot have one without the other. What news we carry with us is the decision we wrestle with daily. When we daily choose wisely, the good news of Jesus Christ will be evident in our lives.

Questions for Reflection:

1. When you enter a room, what atmosphere do you bring?

2. Evaluate your Christian witness; how can Paul's words, "I am not ashamed of the Gospel" become a stronger reality in your life?

3. How can the truths found in this devotional be lived out in your life today?

JUST ONE MORE LOG ON THE FIRE

"We can only afford ourselves one fire, and are obliged to lie without shelter, the nights are cold and days warm." Meriwhether Lewis, April 22, 1806

Imagine being out in the outdoors, night time settles in, and all you want to do is warm up next to a nice big fire. Although Lewis and Clark did this a lot, there were times when, because of the terrain of the land, they simply could not burn all the wood they wanted. Even though the nights were cold, they had to exercise self-control and not burn all the wood they had at one time, because, if they did, they would freeze. In some areas, there simply was not enough wood to allow them to burn fires as big as they wanted.

> *"But the fruit of the Spirit is love, joy, peace, patience, kindness, goodness, faithfulness, gentleness, self-control; against such things there is no law." Galatians 5:22-23*

Self-control does not come easily, for it is "self" that utterly destroys us. "Self" desires nothing but satisfying the cravings of the self, and nothing more. So how can a person control the "self" we have within us? The answer is in the negative...we can't.

We are utterly helpless to achieve self-control, that is, if we try to do it in our own power. It is by the power of the Holy Spirit, as we allow Him to have His control over our lives, that we then are able to exercise self-control. It is because the control is coming, not from our own efforts relying on ourselves, but by our own efforts relying on the leading and guiding of the Spirit.

There is a big difference. One rests its hope in the self. The other rests its hope in the Spirit. Daily choosing to die to ourselves is essential, for when we die to ourselves, then the Holy Spirit is made more alive in us.

Questions for Reflection:

1. How does your inability to defeat "self" empower God's work in your life?

2. In what areas in your life do you need more self-control?

3. How can the truths found in this devotional be lived out in your life today?

CHIEF INFLUENCER

"This Cheif is a man of much influence not only in his own nation but also among the neighbouring tribes and nations." Meriwhether Lewis, April 27, 1806

Lewis and Clark had to be experts at diplomacy for the expedition to succeed. Part of their strategy was understanding the tribal culture of the Indian tribes they encountered. They quickly understood that if they connected with the chief of the tribe, they did not need to worry about problems. The chief was the one who influenced all the others in the tribe.

"He who believes in Me, as the Scripture said, 'From his innermost being shall flow rivers of living water.'" John 7:38

The follower of Jesus is one who embraces and releases influence. He embraces the influence of the Holy Spirit on his life. The influence of the Holy Spirit is welcomed, and it leads to the sanctification of the man.

To embrace the Holy Spirit means to declare that He is the guiding and primary influence in life and to be willing to submit to the influence He freely gives. And that is the challenge: submission to His influence, in spite of the world's scorn. The follower of Jesus is one who also releases influence. When we embrace the influence of the Holy Spirit, then we are able to release godly influence on those around us. This is the pattern influence must take: first influence from Him, then our influence on others.

Questions for Reflection:

1. Think of all the things influencing your life. Where does the Holy Spirit fit in?

2. How does your personal walk with Jesus directly affect how you influence those around you?

3. How can the truths found in this devotional be lived out in your life today?

INVADE A WORLD

"At 10:00 P.M. the dance ended and the nativs retired; they were much gratified in seeing some of our party join them in their dance." William Clark, April 28, 1806

It is hard to imagine how exhausted the men of the Corps of Discovery must have been all the time. To go through such physical labor took a toll on the men. But they could not let their fatigue compromise one major part of the purpose: to build relationships and gather information from Indian tribes. Part of that included staying up far into the night, taking part in the native dances and feasts. They must have been exhausted, but they did it anyway. They entered the cultural world of the native tribes, so they could build relationships. They had to. By doing this, they earned the respect of many of the natives. In reality, they invaded a whole new world for the sake of the bigger picture of the expedition.

> *"But emptied Himself, taking the form of a bondservant, and being made in the likeness of men." Philippians 2:7*

True followers of Christ understand that to reach others, they have to become like others at times and invade their world. Jesus stepped off the throne of heaven and stepped into our sin-soaked, ugly world with the intention of reconciliation. We must do the same.

In order to reach the lost, we have to step into their world at times and invade their world with the light of the Gospel. The darkness says we are not welcome; God says our welcome is never more needed.

To enter others' worlds, we must bring the message of the Father humbling Himself to make Himself known to us. Can we imagine what it was like for a perfect, holy God to come into this world? He did not have to. But he did. And He did it gladly and willingly.

Oh, how we owe our everything to Christ! He became like one of us, yet without sin, and He entered our world. The lost are all around us. What world have you invaded recently with the light of the Gospel?

Questions for Reflection:

1. Taking a look at your life, are there any "worlds" the Lord is asking you to invade?

2. Reflect on the truth of Jesus invading our world. What examples can you take from that amazing example?

3. How can the truths found in this devotional be lived out in your life today?

BLUE GLASS BEADS

"Blue beeds however may form an exception to this remark; This article among all nations of this country may be justly compared to gold and silver among civilized nations." William Clark, May 3, 1806

Trading and exchanging of gifts were the economy of the times with the Indian tribes. Lewis and Clark were well supplied with things to trade, and it was the blue glass beads that seemed to be the hot item among most tribes. Simple blue glass beads were valued by the Indians, and they would trade many things for them.

> *"That the proof of your faith, being more precious than gold which is perishable, even though tested by fire, may be found to result in praise and glory and honor at the revelation of Jesus Christ." 1 Peter 1:7*

Peter gives us an amazing insight. He lets us know that we cannot put a price tag on our faith in Jesus Christ. Our faith is simply too precious to measure.

Often the value of something is measured by what it costs. Our faith in a redeemer cost that very Redeemer His life; therefore, the faith we have in Jesus is truly priceless and cannot be measured. Along with this, it is the "proof" of our faith that Peter deems as more valuable than gold.

What is the proof of our faith to the world? When the world looks at us, what proof do we give them that we follow Jesus? The reason the proof of our faith is so much more precious than gold is because it is *that* proof...that life lived for Christ that draws the lost to Him. To live a life of faith that draws others to Christ is worth more than all the gold in the world.

Questions of Reflection:

1. Faith in Jesus is priceless. How should this affect the way you measure your worth and the worth of others?

2. In what ways do you tend to place higher value on things than you do on your faith in Jesus?

3. How can the truths found in this devotional be lived out in your life today?

WEARING TWO FACES

"The cut nose said that the twisted hair was a bad man and wore two faces..." William Clark, May 8, 1806

To be a man who "wore two faces" in the native culture meant someone who was a hypocrite. Lewis and Clark had to make sure they were not this type of people, for they were trying to lay a foundation of trust with the native tribes, and they needed to be men of their word. As the entry above states, a hypocrite was just as detestable to the Indian as it was to the white man.

> *"Woe to you, scribes and Pharisees, hypocrites! For you clean the outside of the cup and of the dish but inside they are full of robbery and self-indulgence."*
> *Matthew 23:25*

It is easy to read the words of Jesus here and feel as if we were standing next to Him, glaring at the scribes and Pharisees, when all along, it is we who would probably be standing there with them, spoiled and ruined by our own hypocrisy. We all have a "scribe" and a "Pharisee" within us, and we must take heed to Jesus' warning here.

A good indicator of where the scribe and Pharisee lurk within us is when we point them out in the lives of others. We must beware of this. We must beware of the times we find ourselves finding hypocrisy in others, for it is during those times that we find we are the biggest hypocrites. We must treat hypocrisy as we would a rabid animal: we must stay as far away from it as we can.

Questions for Reflection:

1. Take a good look inside yourself. Is there a "scribe" or a "Pharisee"?

2. How does hypocrisy affect the spreading of the Gospel to the lost?

3. How can the truths found in this devotional be lived out in your life today?

ONE DAY...FOUR SEASONS

"At the distance of 18 miles from the river and on the Eastern border of the high plain the Rocky Mountain commences and presents us with Winter. Here we have Summer, Spring, and winter in the short space of twenty or thirty miles." William Clark, May 17, 1806

The dreaded Rocky Mountains were the nemesis of the expedition. Though beautiful and majestic, they caused all sorts of problems, and the men worried constantly about crossing them. Memories of almost starving to death the previous winter weighed heavily on their minds. To top it off, the harsh weather conditions were completely unpredictable. It seemed as if it were a normal thing to experience all four seasons within a short period of time. The frustration of the weather must have weighed heavily on the men; they would wake to a warm sunrise, but bed down in a frigid blizzard.

> *"Jesus Christ is the same yesterday and today, yes and forever." Hebrews 13:8*

In a world of uncertainty, God never changes. He is stable and true, and so are His ways. He gives us two key blessed assurances that stand out above the rest. They are always constant and unyielding to the weather changes of life. These are the love of God and the assurance of His presence. God's love remains the same at any phase in a person's life. It does not change like the weather; it is always unconditional, always unconditional! At the end of the day, it is the need to be loved that man searches for, and it is only through Jesus Christ that that search is brought to an end. Christ completes it.

Man will try one thing this day and something else the next day, all in a search for love. But this search will end only in the emptiness of the soul. The constant love of God is the one true love man can rest in. The other is His presence. It is also never changing. He is with us everywhere, through good and bad. The follower of Christ can go through unimaginable "hell" on earth, because the hell is temporary, but His presence is eternal. It is the certainty of His presence that reminds us we are never alone.

Questions for Reflection:

1. How can you allow the presence of God and the love of God to become more of a reality in your life?

2. In what ways do the daily "weather changes of life" keep you from recognizing God's love and presence?

3. How can the truths found in this devotional be lived out in your life today?

LIGHT EXPOSURE

"A fine day we exposed all our baggage to the sun to air and dry."
William Clark, May 22, 1806

The men were always dealing with the elements. One of the frustrations that "came with the territory" was rain. Rain and moisture caused the men's clothing to rot, their weapons to rust and their food to mold. So when the sun shown, they never passed the opportunity to lay out their supplies to dry and air out. When baggage was put in the light, it dried out and was fit for use again.

> *"And the light shined in the darkness, and the darkness did not comprehend it." John 1:5*

God always uses His divine light of truth to make His followers fit for use. He exposes the baggage we have, and we must allow His light to show it for what it is...nasty baggage.

This is the difference between the redeemed man and the one who has not followed Jesus. One embraces the light to expose his weakness and failures; the other runs from the light to remain in the darkness of sin. One rejoices in his failures, for they force him to rely on the grace of God. The other shuns his failures, for they remind him of his helpless state, though he still does not turn to the light. One desires to be "fit for use" in the bigger picture of God's kingdom; the other desires to be kept in the smaller picture of selfishness.

When we come to the light every day, we will always be fit for use. If we hide in the darkness, we can never be used to the potential God desires for us. The light has to expose our baggage in order to prepare us as messengers.

Questions for Reflection:

1. Do you daily allow God to shed his light upon your sin and cleanse you?

2. Are there areas in your life where you need to stop hiding in the darkness and expose those areas to the light?

3. How can the truths found in this devotional be lived out in your life today?

GOOD HEARTS

"They said that they were pore but their hearts were good. we might be assured of their sincerety." William Clark, May 28, 1806

On their return trip, the men came across the Chopunnish Indians. Trust was everything between the natives and the expedition. Whom to trust...whom not to? The questions were on the men's minds, as well as the Indians'. The above entry gets to the heart of it all: though the Chopunnish were a poor tribe, they assured the Corps of Discovery that they had good hearts and could be trusted.

> *"Then the Lord saw that the wickedness of man was great on the earth, and that every intent of the thoughts of his heart was only evil continually."* Genesis 6:5

The problem every man has to deal with is an "issue of the heart." Man is born with a spiritual "heart disease." Man has tried every way to heal the heart, and every attempt has failed. This is why we cannot ask God to fix our hearts or repair the damage sin has caused.

No, complete healing cannot come this way. The only way our "heart disease" can be cured is with a "heart transplant." This is what Christ does for us: He does not simply *fix* our hearts; He gives us completely new ones, hearts where He can reside. This is the only solution to the issue of the heart.

No matter how good people think their hearts are, unless new hearts are given to them by Christ, their hearts are sick; the illness is terminal. How amazing it is to be given a new heart by the power of God! A heart that is heavenly in its direction and Godly in its convictions!

Questions for Reflection:

1. What is the main problem of the human heart today, no matter how "good" a person may appear to be?

2. What does Jesus do differently than every other false religion in the world when it comes to our hearts?

3. How can the truths found in this devotional be lived out in your life today?

THOSE TREACHEROUS MOUNTAINS

"In order to prepare in the most ample manner in our power to meet that wretched portion of our journey, the Rocky Mountains, where hungar and Cold in their most rigorous form assail the waried travellar; not any of us yet forgotten our sufferings in those mountains in September last, I think it probable we never shall." William Clark, June 2, 1806

Sometimes we need to realize the fears these men had. One of them was the Rocky Mountains. They almost starved to death there once, and, had it not been for the Nez Perce, they surely would have. They finally made it through, only yet again to have to face those treacherous mountains that looked like jagged teeth on the horizon, just waiting to swallow them up. They had to get back east, and the Rockies were in their way. Oh, how the fear, doubt and uncertainty must have crept in!

> *"Then David said to the Philistine, 'You come to me with a sword, a spear, and a javelin, but I come to you in the name of the Lord of hosts, the God of the armies of Israel, whom you have taunted.'" 1 Samuel 17:45*

It is significant to know that David saw four things: Goliath, his sword, his spear and his javelin. David wanted Goliath to know that though Goliath had these man-made things, all David needed was one thing: God. He shows Goliath that not even all the weapons of the Philistines could come against the God of Israel.

This is a timely lesson for any fear the follower of Jesus may have. Nothing, not even the scariest of times, is anything but a small ant to squash before the living God. Though the trials we face may seem like mountains, when we see them through the eyes of God, they are but speed bumps on the road to sanctification.

We need not fear anything, be it trials, disease, or even death, because, in the end, the Word of the Lord is on our side! David saw God in the situation. He did not let the situation define God; he let God define the situation. That is the key. We need to let God define

169

the situation. It is never the other way around. When we let God define the situation, those mountains on the road to sanctification are mere speed bumps. We must let God define every situation we come across.

Questions for Reflection:

1. When difficult times come, do you see God in the situation?

2. Why is it important to let God define the situations that come to us?

3. How can the truths found in this devotional be lived out in your life today?

WAITING ON SNOW

"We have now been detained near five weeks in consequence of the snows; a serious loss of time at this delightfull season for traveling." Meriwhether Lewis, June 14, 1806

Frustration was running high as Lewis and his men were holed up because of snow. They were anxious to get back to the East, but they had to wait for the snow to melt, or disaster would follow.

> *"The Lord is good to those who wait for Him, to the person who seeks Him. It is good that he waits silently for the salvation of the Lord." Lamentations 3:25-26*

Waiting is God's way of humbling us into submission to His perfect will. By nature, we are not creatures of patience, but of impatience. This is why many times God puts us in situations where His only voice is silence, and His only command is to wait. He has His reasons, and when we desire to move forward when He is asking us to wait, we forge into dangerous territory He does not want us to be in.

When we wait, we learn to depend on God. When we wait, we lay down our own ambitions and commit them to God. When we wait, we realize how helpless we are without His timing. We must look at waiting on God as we would a morning sunrise, a time of peace, quiet and beauty. The more we learn to wait, the more colors of His perfect timing come to life before our eyes.

Questions for Reflection:

1. What attitude should you have during times of waiting on the Lord?

2. What would be the purpose of God not answering your prayers when you want them answered?

3. How can the truths found in this devotional be lived out in your life today?

TRUSTED GUIDE

"But returning to the quawmash flatts we shall sooner be informed wheather or not we can procure a guide to conduct us thorugh the Mountains." William Clark, June 20, 1806

Few things were more valuable in the Bitterroot Mountains than a trusted guide. Lewis and Clark knew they needed a guide to get through, because their first attempt to get through the mountains ended in failure. The guide was a person they would lean on and trust without hesitation to lead them through those dreaded mountains. A guide had to know what was in the best interest of the party to make that trip.

> *"But when He, the Spirit of truth, comes, He will guide you into all the truth." John 16:13*

Perhaps one of the biggest mistakes the Christian makes is not recognizing that the Holy Spirit is our constant guide and has promised to be with us always. We try to navigate through life, testing every road except the one we already have had promised to us by the Holy Spirit.

He is our dependable guide for whom we never have to search, because He is within us all the time and desires to guide us into truth in all things. In every situation, He guides us, not in the way we want to go or to the things we desire to see, but He guides us to the way of *His* plan, desiring that we see the truth.

So many fail to utilize the guidance of the Holy Spirit. We do not see that He is our guide and will indeed guide us! Do we want to be guided into all truth? Or do we want to be guided into our own fogged concept of what we *think* is truth? No! It must be our innermost desire to lean on our guide, the Holy Spirit, and follow Him into truth!

173

Questions of Reflection:

1. When it comes to making decisions, how often do you rely on the Holy Spirit?

2. What things in life tend to guide you instead of the Holy Spirit?

3. How can the truths found in this devotional be lived out in your life today?

COMPANIONS

"I took leave of my worthy friend and companion Capt. Clark and the party that accompanyed him. I could not avoid feeling much concern on this occasion although I hoped this seperation was only momentary." Meriwhether Lewis, July 3, 1806

One can only imagine the deep companionship that Lewis and Clark had. On their return trip, they parted ways for a while, and it must have been a sobering time for both of them. They decided to split their party, explore different areas and meet up again at a later date. This was a huge risk. For all they knew, they might never see each other again. They had lived life together, braved dangers together, and overcome impossible odds together. Companions to the end they were.

> *"Now after this the Lord appointed seventy others, and sent them two by two ahead of Him to every city and place where He Himself was going to come." Luke 10:1*

We were designed for companionship. First, we were designed for companionship with the Lord. That is our ultimate relationship. He promises to never leave us nor forsake us because He knows our innermost need for this. He shows His true Father-heart to us.

As we should be rooted in this, we then have the second design play out in our need for companionship with others. When we look to the Scriptures, we do not in any way see a model of ministry that says, "Do it by yourself." We need others to further the kingdom of Christ.

We should take notice of the fact that Jesus sent them out in twos. We must realize two very important things. First, God has placed others in our lives to work alongside us for His eternal purposes. We need to embrace that, even if it means taking the hard road of discipleship. The second truth we must grasp is that though our companions here on earth will fail us, disappoint us, and often hurt us, we have the Holy Spirit who will never do any of that, but

175

will be our companion through thick and thin, from now to forevermore.

Questions for Reflection:

1. When you look at your life, how much of your mentality is "I can do this myself"?

2. What ways are you striving to work with others to further God's kingdom?

3. How can the truths found in this devotional be lived out in your life today?

THANKFUL FOR PROVIDENCE

"These bear are a most tremendous animal; it seems that the hand of providence has been most wonderfully in our favor with rispect to them, or some of us would long since have fallen a sacrifice to their farosity." Meriwhether Lewis, July 15, 1806

The grizzly bear was a very real danger to the Corps of Discovery, when they had several dangerous encounters with it. It is interesting that Lewis attributed the fact that nobody on the expedition had become bear food as a direct result of the protection of Providence. He actually took time to recognize that maybe something bigger than they was deserving of thanks in the success of their expedition. As he jotted down this journal entry, we can only imagine how truly thankful he must have been, considering the numerous dangers they had come across due to the grizzly bear.

> *"Surely the righteous will give thanks to Thy name; The upright will dwell in Thy presence." Psalm 140:13*

The Christian life is, first of all, a life lived with a process of thankfulness. It starts from thankfulness for what we have been delivered from. Then it progresses into thankfulness for the realization of who we now are in Christ. This then leads us to being able to be thankful for the person we are becoming through the Holy Spirit. This then points us to the thankfulness for what we one day will be.

What a beautiful progression of divine thankfulness! When we strive to stay thankful, we cannot but worship Him for whom our thanks is given. As we see His work in our lives from beginning to what one day will be an end, the two words that shout forth are "Thank you!"

Questions for Reflection:

1. Does your life typically show a lifestyle of thankfulness to God?

2. In what areas of your life can you begin to become more grateful to God?

3. How can the truths found in this devotional be lived out in your life today?

MEETING AT THE FIRE

"This morning at daylight the indians got up and crouded around the fire." Meriwhether Lewis, July 27, 1806

The fire was a central point where the men gathered, talked, dreamed of reaching the Pacific, and dreamed of loved ones at home. It was a place to warm up in the morning and evening. Most of the time, it was a peaceful place where men could relax. The entry above describes the moments just before two Blackfeet Indians were killed by Lewis and his men. As the Indians crowded around the fire, they noticed one of the men had left his gun lying around. When they tried to steal it, all hell broke loose, and two men were dead. They would be the only people to die from violence on the entire expedition. The fire, a place typically for warmth and fellowship, had become a place of death.

> *"And so when they got out upon the land, they saw a charcoal fire already laid, and fish placed on it, and bread." John 21:9*

Peter denied Jesus three times...and every time he did it he was standing around a fire. The fire was a place where Peter abandoned Jesus. After Jesus died, He rose again, and we see that He chose to meet Peter where? In a temple? In a village? In a market? No. He chose to meet Peter around a fire, the same place where Peter had abandoned Him.

This is the Gospel. Jesus meets us in the very place we have abandoned Him. Peter smelled the smoke of the fire and was filled with shame. Jesus smelled the smoke of the fire and was filled with compassion, forgiveness and grace. This is the God we serve, One who meets us in the very place we abandoned Him.

<u>Questions for Reflection</u>:

1. What fire does Jesus want to meet you at today?

2. Why does Jesus meet us in those areas we are ashamed of?

3. How can the truths found in this devotional be lived out in your life today?

CORRODED VESSEL

"Having now nothing to detain us we passed over immediately to the island in the entrance of Maria's river to launch the red perogue, but found her so much decayed that it was impossible with the means we had to repare her and therefore mearly took the nails and other ironworks about her which might be of service to us and left her." Meriwhether Lewis, July 28, 1806

On their return trip, Lewis and his men came to the mouth of the Marias River where they had stored a pirogue (a small canoe), that they used on the trip west. It had been quite a while since they had buried it, and the weather and elements had corroded it to the point where it was of no use. Natural corrosion destroyed the vessel.

"Then when lust has conceived, it gives birth to sin; and when sin is accomplished, it brings forth death."
James 1:15

No sin simply appears. It is never that way. The sin that happens in the life of a believer is the result of something that has been rusting over a period of time within the soul. The act of sinning is the rotten fruit of a long term inner corrosion of the soul.

We were not designed to have sin inhabit us, but it does. Therefore, our natural desire is to corrode our soul, not to nourish it. We may call it "natural corrosion of the soul." This is where we must look to the power of the Holy Spirit to reveal the corrosion that is going on in us, so we can kill it immediately.

We are creatures of pattern. We may choose which pattern our lives will live by: patterns that lead to our corrosion or patterns that lead to our sanctification. Which will we choose? If we choose the patterns of corrosion of the soul, then we must never be surprised at the extreme sins we fall into. How foolish we are when we act surprised. However, if we choose patterns of sanctification, we may rejoice in the amazing abundant life and victories we experience through the work of the Holy Spirit.

181

Questions for Reflection:

1. What "corrosion" are you allowing in your life that gives birth to sin?

2. Why is it important to have healthy patterns in your life?

3. How can the truths found in this devotional be lived out in your life today?

LIFE OR DEATH

"I encouraged them by telling them that our own lives as well as those of our friends and fellow travellers depend on our excersions at this moment; they were allert soon prepared the horses and we again resumed our march." Meriwhether Lewis, July 28, 1806

The only bloodshed on the entire expedition happened when Lewis and his men killed two Blackfeet Indians who were trying to steal their guns. As soon as that happened, Lewis knew that if they did not get out of Blackfoot country and meet up with Clark and his men, they were dead men. They had to ride harder, walk faster and move more quickly now than at any point in their expedition. This entry shows how concerned Lewis was about the reality that he and his men were truly in a life or death situation.

> *"Then the Lord God formed man of the dust from the ground, and breathed into his nostrils the breath of life; and man became a living being." Genesis 2:7*

Without God, man is dead. With God, man becomes alive. Following Jesus is truly a matter of life and death. This is brought to reality in two main ways. The first deals with the eternal destiny of the souls of man. To follow Jesus, one steps from death to life in eternity. This is the single most important time in a person's life, the time when he truly realizes that to live without a Savior is indeed a death sentence for eternity...forever. There is no second chance after death. Without Jesus, man is doomed.

The other way is when, once redeemed, a Christian's daily walk with Jesus is indeed another matter of life and death. Unless we abide in Him, we cannot bring forth any life-bearing good fruit. We were meant to be connected with Jesus; He has done His part to make that possible, and we must do ours through prayer, Bible study, fellowship, etc. This is what produces life within us.

We often teeter as "dead" followers of Jesus because we do not abide in Him. Though saved, our light to the lost is dull and dusty...ineffective. Let us beware of being dead Christians and

183

realize that our relationship with Jesus is truly a matter of daily life and death.

Questions for Reflection:

1. What does it mean to be "alive in Christ"?

2. In what ways do you daily allow Jesus to live in and through you?

3. How can the truths found in this devotional be lived out in your life today?

HIDING FROM THE TRUTH

"I asked him whether he did not hear me when I called to him so frequently which he absolutely denied. I do not believe that the fellow did it intentionally but after finding that he had shot me was anxious to conceal his knowledge of having done so." Meriwhether Lewis, August 11, 1806

While hunting elk, Private Peter Cruzatte accidentally shot Lewis in the leg. Probably out of fear, he covered up his actions, stating he had not done it. Although he may have been telling the truth, it was obvious from the ball found in Lewis' leg that it was from Cruzatte's gun. Cruzatte covered up his mistake and hid from the truth rather than admit it.

> *"And there is no creature hidden from His sight, but all things are open and laid bare to the eyes of Him with whom we have to do." Hebrews 4:13*

One day, we will be held accountable for every word we have spoken, every thought we have thought, and every deed we have done. It is foolish for us to think that our "secret sins" are secret. Indeed, they are the most exposed of all!

Though they may be hidden from the eyes of man, they are always before the eyes of God where nothing is hidden. Indeed, they are before the face of God daily, and, like a terrible flash that damages the retinas of an eye, our sin hurts the heart of God over and over and over.

We were not made to hide our sin, but to let His divine light expose us to His healing grace. What if we actually grasped the truth that *nothing* is hidden before His eyes! No thought, no word, no deed. How would our lives be different if we simply understood this?

God's desire is not to be Big Brother, glaring over our shoulders waiting for us to mess up, but His desire is that His omnipresent nature would help us understand that He truly cares for us and knows what is best for us. His watchful eye provides safety, security and divine guidance, leading to truth and sanctification.

Questions for Reflection:

1. Are there any sins that you are "hiding" from God right now?

2. How should the truth that He knows every thought, word, and deed about us transform our daily lives?

3. How can the truths found in this devotional be lived out in your life today?

PROCEEDING ON

"Set out at Sunrise and proceeded on." William Clark, August 14, 1806

The phrase "we proceeded on" is a common theme found in the journals. One foot in front of the other: that was how the Corps of Discovery reached the Pacific. There were no shortcuts; there was no easy way. They simply had to daily choose to put one foot in front of the other and move forward. They had to choose to "proceed on" every minute of every day, because that was how they would achieve their goal. Sure, there were setbacks and disappointments, but they understood that that was all part of the process of proceeding on.

> *"I press on toward the goal for the prize of the upward call of God in Christ Jesus." Philippians 3:14*

The true test of the depth of a man's faith is how he "proceeds on." When we walk with Jesus, we take the responsibility on ourselves to put on His righteousness daily and walk according to His ways.

There is no quick, easy path to following Jesus. It is a daily choice to put Him on and proceed on. Much of the Christian walk is simply this. The twelve disciples did not understand that when the going got tough, they were called to proceed on. Instead, they fled and abandoned their Savior.

Perhaps they did not realize that one of the greatest joys in following Jesus is having Him walk beside us in the monotony of proceeding on toward the higher calling of Christ Jesus. This is a lesson we must learn in our quick, instant gratification culture. There is no room for proceeding on in today's culture, because to proceed on means being content with the everyday joy of simply walking with Him. It is in proceeding on with Jesus step-by-step that we allow Him to be our greatest teacher. It is there we spend time with Him, recognize Him, and allow Him to teach us how to continue. Oh, yes, it is a process, but a marvelous one for us to embrace, not to avoid.

Questions for Reflection:

1. How has today's culture affected you in your process of sanctification?

2. Do you find yourself in a time of "monotony" right now? How are you allowing Jesus to be glorified in that?

3. How can the truths found in this devotional be lived out in your life today?

ADOPTED SONS

"I offered to take his little son a butifull promising child who is 19 months old to which they both himself & wif wer willing provided the child had been weened. they observed that in one year the boy would be sufficiently old to leave his mother & he would then take him to me if I would be so friendly as to raise the child for him in such a manner as I thought proper, to which I agreed &c." William Clark, August 17, 1806

William Clark had a soft spot for Jean Baptiste, the child of Charbonneau and Sacajawea. After spending almost two years with the little fellow, he grew fond of him and asked to take over his parenting. Clark raised him in St. Louis and paid for his future schooling.

> *"He predestined us to adoption as sons through Jesus Christ to Himself, according to the kind intention of His will." Ephesians 1:5*

Adoption is made possible only through the desire, will and effort of the one adopting. A child who is awaiting adoption is utterly helpless, at the mercy of those who want to adopt.

This is the beauty of knowing that we are adopted by Christ. It is only by His amazing grace that we are His followers. He did everything. He did the hard work. He did the choosing. He claimed us as His own. Nothing on our part can boast, for even our desire to follow Him is a gift of His grace.

When we realize we are adopted, what security that brings! For what kind of father would ever un-adopt his children? This process of adoption is meant to reassure us of how much He does love us, how helpless we are without Him, and how much He desires our adoption into His kingdom.

Questions for Reflection:

1. When you think of Christ adopting you, what does that say about His character and your worth?

2. What roles do the one adopting and the one being adopted play in the process?

3. How can the truths found in this devotional be lived out in your life today?

OPEN EARS

"He also gave me near 2 quarts of the Tobacco & informed me he had always had his ears open to what we had said, that he was well convinced that the Seeoux was the cause of all the trouble between the Mandans & them." William Clark, August 21, 1806

Much of the communication between Lewis and Clark dealt not only with speaking, but, more importantly, listening. Whether there were hidden motives or clear ones, both the Indians and Lewis and Clark had to carefully listen to each other while communicating. So much hung in the balance that listening was a key part of success for both parties.

> *"This you know, my beloved brethren. But let everyone be quick to hear, slow to speak and slow to anger." James 1:19*

Listening is often overlooked as one of the most effective methods of evangelism. We often think that talking is the key, when it is indeed listening that opens doors to share the Gospel. We must not forget that the Lord heard the cries of His people, and then He acted.

God is a God who listens. Therefore, as His followers, we must also be people who listen. Listening is powerful, for it shows value to others and challenges us to put aside our own motives and open our hearts to others' hurts. Listening is an area that must be developed, and the only way it can be developed is through practice. And the only way we can practice is by being with people. Jesus spent time with men: he listened to them, and, after listening, He pointed them to the truth. We must do the same.

<u>Questions for Reflection:</u>

1. Do you tend to really listen to people when they talk to you?

2. How does listening show someone the love of Christ and provide a great platform for evangelism?

3. How can the truths found in this devotional be lived out in your life today?

RENAMED

"We landed on the S.W. side and I sent out two men to a village of Barking Squirels to kill some of those animals." William Clark, August 30, 1806

So intrigued were they by this creature that they actually sent one alive back to Thomas Jefferson on their way west. The barking squirrel was later renamed and given the name of "prairie dog."

> *"He brought him to Jesus. Jesus looked at him and said, 'You are Simon the son of John; you shall be called Cephas (which is translated Peter).'" John 1:42*

Simon had a name given to him by his earthly father, but Jesus gave him a new name. Jesus looked deep into the heart of Simon and saw a future Peter. He did not become Peter "the rock" at once; it was a process of sanctification.

That is what Jesus does with us; he renames us according to His purposes. He renames us "forgiven," "righteous," "holy" and "adopted." These are the common names we all take on as we believe in Christ.

Our name has nothing to do with how we see ourselves, because we will always see ourselves as Simons. In truth, our new name is defined by who Jesus says we are, and He looks at us and sees "Peters." He sees a new creation based on His power within us to transform our hurt and broken spirits into beautiful, powerful Christ-exalting ones.

What a privilege to be named by Christ! When Simon took the name Peter, he took on a new identity; it was a Christ-given identity, completely embraced by Christ who named him, despite failures that would come later.

193

Questions for Reflection:

1. How much of your identity is formed around who Jesus says you are?

2. Why is our "renaming" in Christ so important to understand?

3. How can the truths found in this devotional be lived out in your life today?

AGGRESSIVE ANXIOUSNESS

"Our appears extreamly anxious to get on, and every day appears to produce new anxieties in them to get their country and friends."
William Clark, September 9, 1806

The men were close to home. After two years away, their eagerness to return home to see their loved ones created an anxiety that drove them on, as they paddled down the Missouri. They were in the homestretch. They were anxious to finally see their friends, families and homes.

> *"And He gave some as apostles, and some as prophets, and some as evangelists, and some as pastors and teachers..." Ephesians 4:11*

We were all designed with different passions, and each member of the body of Christ is driven to know Jesus in a different way. Each of us has that thing that fuels our passion to grow close to Jesus.

The evangelist is driven for the fruit of seeing souls added to the story of redemption. The teacher is driven to make the Bible understandable to the student. The pastor is driven by the care for and the value of his people. The prophet is driven to declare the words of the Lord. The apostle is driven to see new works of God birthed in diverse ways.

All of these are different callings, with different passions, but all are anxious for the work of God in their diverse callings. We need to find that which makes us anxious for God in our lives, and we need to walk in that calling. This is where we truly come to the life God designed for us.

What is it that drives us on to the higher calling of Christ? What produces in us a more eager anxiety to know Him more? What is it that allows Christ to shine through us the most? We need to find this calling and seize it. We must let nothing get in the way of that which drives us to Jesus!

Questions of Reflection:

1. What are the things that give you life and spur you on to know Jesus more?

2. What is keeping you from passionately embracing those things?

3. How can the truths found in this devotional be lived out in your life today?

ALMOST FORGOTTEN

"This Gentlemen informed us that we had been long Since given out by the people of the US Generaly and almost forgotten, the Preseident of the U. States had yet hopes of us." William Clark, September 17, 1806

As the men had been gone for such a long time, the general population had given up hope for their return. They were probably thought dead and the mission failed. There were those few though who did not give up hope of their return. Thomas Jefferson was one of those men. Imagine the first meeting they had; while many doubted that they were alive, Jefferson stood proud, knowing he had never given up on them.

> *"And He said to him, "'Truly I say to you, today you shall be with Me in Paradise." Luke 23:43*

There is one thing God cannot do, and that is give up on man. No, it is not His way. His love is too profound to comprehend with our natural minds.

That is the gospel story to the sinner. When man, loved ones, friends, family, and society have given up on the sinner, God enters with compassion and saves him. There is no such thing as no hope with God. There is always hope, and He longs for reconciliation with man to the bitter end.

When the thief cried out, Jesus answered with compassion. He did not give up on the sinner, for, even in His hour of utter agony, He reached out with compassion. What a glorious God we serve! This is the truth that transcends the practical logical thinking of man, colliding with the perfect thinking of a compassionate God who never gives up on man.

Questions for Reflection:

1. How should the truth of God's unconditional love transform your daily life?

2. How often do you find yourself "giving up" on certain people?

3. How can the truths found in this devotional be lived out in your life today?

GAZING AND REFLECTING

"Particularly when exposed to the light, the eye ball is much inflaimed and the lid appears burnt with the Sun, the cause of this complaint of the eye I can't account for. from it's sudden appearnce I am willing to believe it may be owing to the reflection of the sun on the water." William Clark, September 19, 1806

One of the physical challenges of the expedition was exposure to the glare of the rivers' water. After a while, day after day of looking at the water began to affect the men's eyes. The glare was simply too strong, causing terrible harm and pain. The more the men gazed upon the reflection of the sun on the water, the more their faces, and in particular their eyes, were affected.

> *"...and they began to recognize them as having been with Jesus." Acts 4:13b*

Have you ever simply looked at a person and you knew he was one who spent time with Jesus? What we look at alters how others look at us. This is what happened to Moses. He looked at God, and it transformed him, and others took notice.

Do we doubt the same happens today when we strive to look upon the face of Jesus daily? When we set our eyes on Jesus and look to him in all ways, others cannot help but notice. We ourselves may not notice it, but others do. And what they see is the redemptive story of Jesus.

Time spent looking at Jesus is never wasted, whether it be in prayer, reading of the Word, meditation, or simply talking to Him. When we do these things, we allow Him to transform our image to be more like Him. The more we do this, the more we reflect Him in our lives, which then offers us more opportunity to point others to Him. What or whom are you looking to right now? What is forming your image? May it always be Jesus! May our lives be so obsessed with gazing upon Him that when others see us, they immediately see the Father!

Questions for Reflection:

1. Looking at your life right now, would you say that you are recognized as one who spends time with Jesus?

2. Does your daily schedule allow time for Jesus?

3. How can the truths found in this devotional be lived out in your life today?

www.ingramcontent.com/pod-product-compliance
Lightning Source LLC
Chambersburg PA
CBHW051825090426
42736CB00011B/1658